Deep Worship

In Heaven!

*Therefore, by Him let us continually offer the sacrifice
of praise to God, that is, the fruit of our lips, giving thanks
to His name. But do not forget to do good and to share,
for with such sacrifices God is well pleased.*

Hebrews 13:15-16 (NKJV)

*Then I looked, and I heard the voice of many angels
around the throne, the living creatures, and the elders;
and the number of them was ten thousand times
ten thousand, and thousands of thousands,*

Revelation 5:11 (NKJV)

Deep Worship In Heaven!

MOMENTS IN HEAVEN
SERIES BOOK 8

DEAN BRAXTON

Braxton Press
PRODUCTIONS

Copyright © 2017 by Dean Braxton

Deep Worship In Heaven

by Dean Braxton

Printed in the United States of America

ISBN 978-0-9978372-3-0

Unless otherwise indicated, Bible quotations are taken from The New King James Version of the Bible. Copyright © 1982

by Thomas Nelson

www.DeanBraxton.com

DEDICATION

*Dedicated to Marilyn Sue Braxton, my wife,
for showing me a person who truly worships
Father God in Spirit and Truth.*

FOREWORD

Deep Worship in Heaven is a book you don't want to miss! When you read it, you are spiritually refreshed. Dean describes his experiences in heaven with lots of details, and it is a very easy-to-read book. He expounds on his worshipful experience in heaven, ways to worship, and much more. In all of this, he frequently shares biblical verses and is very straightforward. I have thoroughly enjoyed reading Dean's book, and I definitely recommend it to anyone, Christian or non-Christian. I was very convicted when I read this book and believe others will be too.

Joy Kinsinger, Student, Age 15
The Institute of Academic Excellence (Home School)
Washington, Illinois

In 2014, I heard about Dean Braxton and his experience of dying for 1 hour and 45 minutes. Pastor Tony Kemp told me that Dean had died, gone to Heaven, and returned to earth. Everyone in my church, God's Temple of Faith in Syracuse, New York, was excited and couldn't wait to hear him speak. In 2015, when I met Dean in a three-day revival at our church, he shared his testimony about his experience in Heaven. When he spoke, he shared about prayers, worship, and seeing Jesus. He also said everything in Heaven was alive and worshipped the Father. As a praise and worship leader, I was listening and taking in a lot, but what touched my spirit the most was the part about everything worshiping the Father. Dean said that when everything in Heaven worshiped, it was from a pure heart.

Now, I feel that worship is a part of our very being. If God created worship and it resides on the inside of us, then we are created to worship Him forever. This means that when we want to show love to our Father, it ought to come oozing from the heart, through our lips with a shout of praise, along with the clapping and waving of our hands. When we show Him true praise through worship, that's when we can receive new insights from Heaven that will help us produce new songs of encouragement, both for us and to bring honor to God. Also, worshiping will cause us to move in spiritual power in this earthly realm.

I believe that this book, *Deep Worship in Heaven*, will help to take you into that spiritual power and will give you new enhancements of understanding of just how important your praise and worship really is. By reading this book, you will come to apprehend that You Truly Were Created to Be a Worshipper Forever!

Donyelle McClain, Worship Minister
God's Temple Of Faith Ministries
Syracuse, New York

In 2011, my husband invited Dean to speak at our church after we heard his amazing Heaven experience on a television program. After being radically impacted by Dean's testimony the first time that he visited, he has returned yearly, imparting to us a deeper revelation of God's love and our Heavenly home. What Dean shares not only gives you a glimpse into the place of Heaven, but it also reveals how you can experience Heaven on earth. I am reminded of the verse, "Your kingdom come, your will be done, on EARTH as it is in HEAVEN" (Matt 6:10, NKJV). Dean's Heaven encounter is confirmed over and over in the Word of God, with scripture references given chapter by chapter.

This life-changing testimony has taken me personally into a place with the Lord, deeper than I've ever been before. You will experience the love of Jesus drawing you deep into living, moving, and having your very existence in Him. "For in Him we live and move and have our being" (Acts 17:28, NKJV).

You'll be swept up into a place of worshipping the Lord in everything you do, every day of your life. You will find yourself with a deeper revelation of your very existence in Him and through Him. It will also take you into a creative, unrestrained expression of love to Him through worship that you never thought was possible on this side of Heaven. This beautiful place of worship will be flowing in and through you!! This book will bring Heaven to earth in reality. You will never be the same as you are plunged into a deeper love relationship with your Heavenly Father. It's what you were made for; it's what you live for. Get ready to be stirred with a passion for your Lord like never before!!

Lynn Frady, Co-Pastor
Oasis Church
Grover Beach, California

CONTENTS

PREFACE

Author Introduction of
Deep Worship In Heaven

In my hospital room, I would meditate on many of the things I had experienced in Heaven after being dead for 1 hour and 45 minutes. Because of those times, I have decided to write a series of books entitled "Moments In Heaven" that give more details about many of the experiences I had in Heaven.

One of the many experiences I meditated on was the worship and praise in which I participated in Heaven with all of God's creation before the Throne of God Almighty.

In the book, *In Heaven! Experiencing The Throne Of God,* I covered briefly what I saw, smelled, heard, felt, and tasted there. All things in Heaven are not only alive, but intelligent, because absolutely everything connected with the Creator is infused with the life force and intelligence of the Creator.

This book is number eight in the series and covers in more detail what it was like for me to be a part of that great "alive" worshipping in praise before the Throne of God. It also gives insight into what I was thinking about at that time of worship.

I am praying that this book will do four things in helping people worship and praise God in a deeper, more heartfelt way.

I am praying this book will:

1. Bring people to a growing intimacy with God. Every time we praise Him, we will experience new love from Him and for Him.

2. Encourage and inspire new songs to be produced by Christian music artists.

3. Help us understand that worship is being produced in the smallest movement of our body when we praise Him. Even practicing to praise Him in song is always real worship to Him because true worship is not a show.

4. Help us to realize that worship is always personal between us and God. He always sees it that way. He sees you loving Him and Him loving you.

I hope you as the reader experience joy in reading my book, but also try to incorporate worship in all you do! Thanks for taking the time to read *Deep Worship In Heaven.*

Dean A. Braxton

ACKNOWLEDGMENTS

I would like to give special thanks to the following people, who helped to review this book, *Deep Worship In Heaven*. May their suggestions enhance the spiritual growth and understanding of those who read it. I believe it will bring you a level of enjoyment and love only Father God can give. Again to all those that helped, A Sincere Thank You.

Jon Barnard, Barnard Ministries
Portland, Oregon

Pamela Bolton, Pastor
Out of the Box Worship Center
Whitehall, New York

Dave Brooks, WCIC Station Manager
Co-Founder, Three O'clock Session
Peoria, Illinois

Jason Carter, Musician
Chicago, Illinois

Rebecca Cruz, Student
Cuesta College
Arroyo Grande, California

Deborah (Dale) Golder, Worship Leader, Evangelistic Ministries
Lakewood, Washington

John Graves, Chess Coach
Puyallup, Washington

Genesis Hall, Licensed Clinical Social Worker (LCSW),
Therapist, Bloomington, Illinois

Pamela Hart, Grateful Worshiper
Arroyo Grande, California

Chuck Insley, Minister
Portland, Oregon

Jesse Kinsinger, Student
Washington Community High School Washington, Illinois

Junior Mayen, Worship Leader
Manassas, Virginia

Brian & Alisha Richardson, Ministers
Design Developers—Dream Designs, LLC
El Paso, Illinois

Mary Vance, Retired Teacher
Farmer City, Illinois

Katherine Michelle Vincent
Christian Mom and Wife
Tygh Valley, Oregon

Andrea Whiston, Associate Pastor
True Church
Hannibal, Missouri

And finally, I want to thank Tammy Haywood, Music Minister of By His Word Christian Center, Tacoma, Washington. She was the first person who approached me wanting to know details about worship in Heaven. She then asked me to speak at a music rehearsal and share with her team of worship leaders the details and the experience of what it was like to worship God in Heaven.

CHAPTER 1

Worship Causes True Rest!

The Beat of Heaven

The sound, the beat of worship and praise, was still beating as I was at the feet of Jesus. It was like no other beat that I had ever heard. It seemed to be a beat that pulled everything together. I knew it was not God's heart beating or Jesus' heart. It was not a beat coming from the Holy Spirit, who resided on the inside of me. I knew that every creation of God, every being in Heaven, was connected to that beat and enjoyed the connection. The link to the beat had always been surrounding us. The rhythm is linked to us who are joined to Jesus and always will be attached. It was an eternally repeated sound. It was such a perfect beat. All at once, the beat took on a faster pace than when I had first entered into Heaven. It was quicker than at any time I had been in Heaven. I had not moved from the feet of Jesus as the beat was sounding. I looked into His face and into His eyes. I could see the sound coming from His eyes. I understood that it was love coming from His very essence, from Father God's very nature connecting to the Holy Spirit's life within me.

Jesus Moving Away from Me

Jesus looked down at me with such love and then started to move away from me. He did not say a word, but with His eyes, I knew He would be back. As I watched Him move away from me, I wanted to go with Him, but I knew that I was to stay where I was. He no longer stood before me, but was moving toward the Throne of God. He was walking towards the Throne to be with His Father, my Father, and our Father. The beat seemed to get louder with every step He took. Everything around me was so alive. Now, everything around me had changed its focus as we watched together, Jesus moving toward our Father.

The Throne

All of a sudden, the colors around me were changing and were getting brighter around the Throne that was suspended up in the atmosphere. Light and life, surrounding Almighty God, were intensifying. All I knew was that everything that was alive around me was watching Jesus move toward the Throne of God. As He got closer to the Throne, the Throne became brighter with brilliant white lights. It reminded me of a sunrise of white lights. These bright rays around the Throne seemed to strengthen into one color of white as Jesus moved closer. It is hard to tell you just how bright the glory around the Throne became. All I saw was a beautiful, blazing, brilliant light, like lights within a light, within lights around the Throne of God.

Flames of Fire

As Jesus moved even closer to the Throne, I saw the flames of fire before the Throne of God seem to become larger with every step He made towards the Throne. These were part of the brightness I experienced watching the lights around the Throne. They were not all of the reason the light around the Throne got whiter, but they were a part of these beautiful lights. How large they became, I could not tell you. They seemed to be pillars of fire to me, but yet, they were more than that. They were alive and moved in a motion like real people. They did not look like people, but moved like them.

I remember when I first met with Jesus and looked at the Throne of God; I saw them. My connecting with these flames of fire was not new. It was like I had been linked to them for a long time. I knew the joining took place the day I became born again. I knew that these must be the Seven Spirits of God before the Throne.

Now this moment as I saw Jesus moving closer to the Throne of God, the flames of fire were showing a different type of flaming joy and life; and I knew I was a part of that change. As Jesus was in front of this glory of fire, they were glowing larger than ever.

Every Creation in Heaven Honored Jesus

As Jesus moved, I remembered how everything moved out of His way. I saw trees, flowers, grasses, hills, mountains, and even atmospheres move out of His way in respect and bow. I saw rivers of living water stop flowing as He came near so that He could cross their paths on holy ground.

Even the light seemed to be moving out of His way, and at the same moment, the light appeared to be moving before Him. As the lights moved before Him, the light was announcing to all that He was coming their way. He was leaving one form of light and creating another kind of light. The light He created, in His movement toward the Throne, also seemed to make a pathway ahead of Him, like sun rays coming from Him to the

Throne and from the Throne back to Him. His path appeared to become brighter and more brilliant as He moved closer to Father God on the Throne and through the light.

Holy Expectation

The holiness that was on every creation's face, every being of life in heaven, and everything that had life, I cannot describe in words. All I knew was that everything in Heaven had an expectation and an anticipation of something glorious that was about to happen. And it did!

In the Hospital

While I was in my bed in the hospital, I remember how this scene played over and over in my mind. The memories seemed to have a life of their own, as I went over every detail. It was like I was still there, even though I knew I was in the hospital in my bed. As I focused on each particular fact of the experience, I could recall how detailed everything was over and over again. Within each detail is a story in itself. I remember thinking that the scenes I experienced in Heaven were made for all to enjoy. I want all the people on this planet to go there.

The details of the flowers as they watched Jesus reach the Throne of the Father will always be hard for me to describe in words. The particulars of the mountains as they moved with great majesty from in front of Jesus will also be hard to put into words. I remember the music that seemed to be in everything in Heaven with its joyful and peaceful serenity and exhortation sound. I knew that this music was so fulfilling that food was not even a thought in my mind. People were coming into my room at the hospital, and even as I was engaging with them, I was still involved with the scenes of worship in Heaven. I was thinking, "How could this be?" I was with others on this planet, and yet, I was with my Father God and Jesus in Heaven.

I remember reading in the Bible how it talked about entering into His rest. It was something that I had always longed for, but I never really understood what the writer of Hebrews had meant by "enter into the rest of Jesus." And yet now, I had this total experience of rest. Some may call it peace. Some may look at it as serenity, but to me, all I could call this experience was His rest. I just remember saying to myself, "Oh, that's what You mean by Your rest!"

As I said earlier, there I was in the hospital, experiencing all of this as if I was still in Heaven.

HEBREWS 4:8-12 (NKJV)

For if Joshua had given them rest, then He would not afterward have spoken of another day. There remains therefore a rest for the people of God. For he who has entered His rest has himself also ceased from his works as God did from His. Let us therefore be diligent to enter that rest, lest anyone fall according to the same example of disobedience. For the word of God is living and powerful, and sharper than any two-edged sword, piercing even to the division of soul and spirit, and of joints and marrow, and is a discerner of the thoughts and intents of the heart.

Where it reads, "There remains therefore a rest for the people of God," the Greek word here for rest is "Sabbatismós," which is the celebratory expression of the Sabbath or Shabath.

Shabath: (Hebrew origin) make or cause to cease, celebrate, fail, keep, rest, rid, still, desist, take away, put away, leave, or suffer to be lacking.

Pondering for Years

I had pondered for years on how to enter into that rest and what it was. I wanted to enter, but I had no understanding of what it was or how to do it. So, I gave up on it; and then as I lay in the hospital, I said to myself, "Wow! This is that rest!"

Rest was worshipping God! In thinking to myself, everything in Heaven was praising God with all they had. Anything that we did, even the movements we made, was worship.

There was no one saying, "Let's go to worship." There was no one wondering if we would have worship today. There was no one saying, "There is worshipping over there." Everything was praising God in every single moment.

Their actions were worship; their thoughts were worship; their gestures to each other were worship. Worship was always surrounding us with pure love for God Almighty. Worship and rest were one in the same. Now I understood why it was so hard for me to enter into His rest. Worship was doing the will of God; that is what He always wanted from me. In John the 4th chapter in verses 23 through 24, it says that we can experience true worship even now.

JOHN 4:21-24 (NKJV)

Jesus said to her, "Woman, believe Me, the hour is coming when you will neither on this mountain, nor in Jerusalem, worship the Father. You worship what you do not know; we know what we worship, for salvation is of the Jews. But the hour is coming, and now is, when the true worshipers will worship the Father in spirit and truth; for the Father is seeking such to worship Him. God is Spirit, and those who worship Him must worship in spirit and truth."

That Rest

I had always tried to enter into that rest with my abilities. I had always sought to come into worship with my thoughts. I was not praising God in my spirit, but I was worshipping in my flesh. Now by having this experience of being separated from my body because I died, I praised my Father in my spirit with the Spirit of Holiness. I worshipped in real love for my Father. I, now on earth, worship Him in Spirit and Truth from my heart as everything in Heaven did. I had finally entered into His rest through worshipping Him.

PSALM 23:1-6 (NKJV)

The Lord is my shepherd; I shall not want. He makes me to lie down in green pastures; He leads me beside the still waters. He restores my soul; He leads me in the paths of righteousness For His name's sake. Yea, though I walk through the valley of the shadow of death, I will fear no evil; For You are with me; Your rod and Your staff, they comfort me. You prepare a table before me in the presence of my enemies; You anoint my head with oil; My cup runs over. Surely goodness and mercy shall follow me All the days of my life; And I will dwell in the house of the Lord Forever.

.

CHAPTER 2

Worship Is Only For The True God

His Presence Loved Me

As Jesus moved toward the Throne of my Father, I could still look at Him, and oh, how I knew I loved Him. I knew that everything about Him loved me, even as He moved toward the Throne. I just remember how much His presence still had love for me. Even though He moved away from me, I still could say that everything about Him loved me. I looked at everything else, and everything else seemed to be having the same experience that I was having as He went past them. He loved each of them like each was the only one He loved. All I could do as I watched Him move away from me was experience a sense of great anticipation for what was about to take place. I had sensed great joy coming from Jesus. I experienced the gladness of everything around me. I knew that this blissfulness we all were in was because of a huge moment that was about to happen.

The Father

As I looked at my Father, I saw the glory that was coming off of Him. His glory looked like streams of red, white, blue, orange, yellow, green, purple, violet, turquoise, and more. There were also so many other colors of lights coming off of Him that I could not name. He was creating new colors every moment. All of the colors were alive and bounced around. They reminded me of birds that I had seen jumping up and down as they looked for food in a field of grass. These colors also were indwelled with great love for everything that they came in contact with. I remember them coming and swirling around me as I was on my hands and knees, looking toward my God, as Jesus was about to enter into His Father's Glory.

Love and Joy of Jesus

All I could remember was the love and joy that was coming from Jesus, my Father, and everything else there in Heaven. I, myself, was vibrating with joy. Everything in me wanted to jump out of me and just praise Jesus and my Father. Even the Holy Spirit who was living on the inside of me was vibrating.

In the Hospital

As I thought about it later in my hospital room, I could understand now, how some people, when they give God their whole being, have such a presence of God around them that they cannot stand on their own two feet. I came to a conclusion about myself. My flesh could not have stood the vibration of the Holy Spirit that lived on the inside of me. My flesh no longer could be a part of what it was not naturally made to participate in, the fullness of life there in Heaven. It could not join the full praising of God, my Father, and Jesus, my Lord, and Savior.

Jesus Enters God's Glory

Back in Heaven, I remember the Holy Spirit pulling me into this beautiful atmosphere of worship and praise. I knew at that moment that I was going to praise the Lord with everything that I was created of. I kept looking at Jesus as He started to ascend upward toward the Throne in the heavenly atmosphere. As He moved toward my Father, I realized that He, Jesus, was not planning on stopping at God's almighty Throne. He walked right up to my Father and disappeared within the glory of God. The fiery pillars that were before the Throne, followed Him in. It was like Jesus became the Father's Glory. It was like He melted right into the Father God. When Jesus had entered into the Father, it was like I entered too. I knew what the statement meant when Jesus said, "I and the Father Are One" (John 10:30).

When I see Jesus, I see the Father. The Father and Jesus are One. Jesus is in the Father, and the Father is in Jesus. I was in the Father, and the Father was in me. Jesus was in me, and I was in Jesus.

I knew that every creation in Heaven was experiencing the same thing that I was experiencing. I was one with the Father, because Jesus was one with the Father. I was one with my Father; I was one with Jesus; I also was one with the Holy Spirit; and they were one with me. When Jesus was entering the Father, the actions of love also entered with Him. Because of this, I wanted to give all the praise I had at that moment to My God!

Back at the Hospital

I remember being in my hospital room, thinking about that moment in which Jesus disappeared within the glory of the Father. As I pondered over what had taken place, I thought to myself that I would never have believed what I had seen if someone had told me that would happen. It was not part of my belief system. I did not know that this would occur in Heaven. I remember that Jesus said in John the 14th chapter, that when you saw Him, Jesus, that you saw His Father. I remember Him saying He was in the Father and the Father was in Him. I remember Him saying that He did not do anything unless the Father showed Him. But now these statements meant much more to me, because I experienced Jesus entering into the Father, my Father. I understood the impact of becoming a full servant of God in worship and praise.

I had become a part of that oneness with God which helped me through the Holy Spirit to change into a complete bond-servant or better yet, to give myself over to worshipping and praising God Almighty in all I do.

I CORINTHIANS 10:31 (NKJV)

Therefore, whether you eat or drink, or whatever you do, do all to the glory of God.

Glory (Greek): honor, praise, worship.

COLOSSIANS 3:17 (NKJV)

And whatever you do in word or deed, do all in the name of the Lord Jesus, giving thanks to God the Father through Him.

Thanks (Greek): to express gratitude.

JOHN 14:8-14 (NKJV)

Philip said to Him, "Lord, show us the Father, and it is sufficient for us." Jesus said to him, "Have I been with you so long, and yet you have not known Me, Philip? He who has seen Me has seen the Father; so how can you say, 'Show us the Father'? Do you not believe that I am in the Father, and the Father in Me? The words that I speak to you I do not speak on My own authority; but the Father who dwells in Me does the works. Believe Me that I am in the Father and the Father in Me, or else believe Me for the sake of the works themselves. Most assuredly, I say to you, he who believes in Me, the works that I do he will do also; and greater works than these he will do, because I go to my Father. And whatever you ask in My name, that I will do, that the Father may be glorified in the Son. If you ask anything in My name, I will do it."

Father's Glory

I had no idea that Jesus would be entering into the Father and becoming the glory of the Father and that the Father would become Him. This was outside of my belief system. This was outside of my knowledge. This was outside of anything I could ever come up with. When He entered in, I knew that I had the right to be in Heaven because of what Jesus did. His dying on the cross, paying my price, and dying my death gave me the legality of being in Heaven. Jesus had the right to enter into the glory of the Father. Because He did that, He gave me the right to be in the Glory of Heaven; His Glory.

I remember in that room in the hospital how I was going over this and the overwhelming rest I was experiencing in Jesus. I understood when He said that He and the Father are one. I knew what that meant. We on this planet have no idea the magnitude of the statement that He made when He said, "The Father and I are One. When you see Me you see the Father." I became eligible by what He did on the cross to have God the Father, Jesus my Lord and Savior, through the Holy Spirit become a part of me forever. They are One and reside in me forever.

What more could I ask for? What more could I want? What more could I want to experience? God Almighty lives on the inside of me. When Jesus entered into the Father, I knew this. All of Heaven knew this. Every angel and every creature created by God knows this. Everything on this planet knows that when we accept Jesus Christ as Lord and Savior, we are truly the sons and daughters of God, the true offspring of God Almighty. We are not only made to look like Him, but also to have Him live within us and us in Him. Even Satan and all his evil spirits know this!

JOHN 17:20-23 (NKJV)

"I do not pray for these alone, but also for those who will believe in Me through their word; that they all may be one, as You, Father, are in Me, and I in You; that they also may be one in Us, that the world may believe that You sent Me. And the glory which You gave Me I have given them, that they may be one just as We are one: I in them, and You in Me; that they may be made perfect in one, and that the world may know that You have sent Me, and have loved them as You have loved Me."

PSALM 18:30-36 (NKJV)

As for God, His way is perfect; The word of the Lord is proven; He is a shield to all who trust in Him. For who is God, except the Lord? And who is a rock, except our God? It is God who arms me with strength, And makes my way perfect. He makes my feet like the feet of deer, And sets me on my high places. He teaches my hands to make war, So that my arms can bend a bow of bronze. You have also given me the shield of Your salvation; Your right hand has held me up, Your gentleness has made me great. You enlarged my path under me, So my feet did not slip.

CHAPTER 3

Worship Plus God Equals Action

Made to Give Pure Praises

As Jesus Himself disappeared or melted into the Father, all of a sudden, the Father Himself was more magnificent. He always stood out, but as Jesus entered into Him, it was like He became even more of the center of everything.

I came to know or gain a different understanding of how nothing can exist without Him, without my Father. All of creation knows this and has always known this. Everything that I was created of came into a greater understanding of my Creator and my being created. I understood. I was perfectly made to give Him pure praise. I knew that original praise comes from within me, because He made me that way. The natural thing for me to do was to praise Him for creating me and to understand that I exist to have real fellowship with Him forever. I existed to have Him in me forever. Everything about me existed to exalt my Creator and to thank Him for creating me with all that I was at that moment with no flaws at all. Now praising Him was what every being there, every creation there, everything that existed there in Heaven knew.

We all had the same agenda, and that was to worship God Almighty forever.

The beat of Heaven seemed to be even louder when Jesus was one with the Father. I was not surprised that it all worked this way. It was like I always had this information in me through the Holy Spirit.

No Sound in Heaven

Every creation in Heaven seemed to be moving with each and every beat. It was like an earthquake taking place, and yet there was no destruction at all. If anything it seemed like everything was edified or enhanced even more with the love of God.

Then, suddenly without any notice, the beat stopped! There was no sound. At the same moment that the beat stopped making a sound, all of creation was quiet. Everything in Heaven was quiet. As I looked around things were still moving, but there was no sound. Even the beat seemed to keep beating, but there was no sound. The sound seemed not to exist at all at that moment. I saw grasses moving like the wind was blowing over them on a very sunny day, but there was no sound. I saw the flowers looking as though they were still moving to the light of the Son, and yet there was no sound. The mountains of Heaven were moving like ocean waves coming on a beach, but there was no sound. For myself, I was still experiencing everything about me vibrating in praise for my Father in the name of Jesus with the help of the Holy Spirit, but there was no sound. Everything in Heaven from the atmosphere to the ground, from angel to angel, from the Redeemed to the animals; all of the creations of God in Heaven were moving, but there was no sound. There was no sound coming from any of them or anything.

A Foundation of Silence

I was not amazed. I knew that this is what was supposed to happen. No sound in Heaven always preceded a great event. All the creations of God and I were anticipating what was to come next. For we all knew the next thing that would take place in Heaven would produce a new sound. It was like we were going to build on the sound that had been with a new sound to come. I knew there had to be no sound for that building to take place. It was this silence that was to be a foundation for a new sound. I knew that at that moment God Almighty would create in each of us, all His creation, a new song. It would be a life-giving sound from God through His children, His creation, us. This was about to happen and before it would take place there had to be silence in Heaven. Even though things were still moving and usually producing sound, no sound was produced. It was like at that moment sound did not exist.

A Shift in Heaven

I knew that something was going to take place in time on the earth, with this new quietness that was created by God. It was like this quiet shift in Heaven was producing a new direction on earth of how God was accomplishing something on the planet.

In the Hospital

Later on, I was in my hospital room pondering over this event of no sound. I asked myself, "Whenever God is getting ready to make a great move that will impact this planet, does all sound in Heaven stop?" Then I remembered that in the book of Revelation there is a moment when there was no sound in Heaven. John states that there was silence in Heaven for half an hour.

REVELATION 8:1-5 (NKJV)

When He opened the seventh seal, there was silence in heaven for about half an hour. And I saw the seven angels who stand before God, and to them were given seven trumpets. Then another angel, having a golden censer, came and stood at the altar. He was given much incense, that he should offer it with the prayers of all the saints upon the golden altar which was before the throne. And the smoke of the incense, with the prayers of the saints, ascended before God from the angel's hand. Then the angel took the censer, filled it with fire from the altar, and threw it to the earth. And there were noises, thunderings, lightnings, and an earthquake.

Silences Outside of Time

There is no way that I can tell you how long this silence lasted that I experienced in Heaven. If I were try to place that moment of silence in time, I feel like I would be lying to you. When I was in Heaven, time was not there. I was in eternity that has no measurement like time. There is no day or night, as in Revelation 2:23 and 22:5. God lights up everything. So how long something took to accomplish, I cannot tell you. The silence seemed very long, and yet, it also appeared to be very short at the same moment.

I just knew a silent movement in Heaven preceded great movements of God that took place on earth. It was like the moment before no longer existed and a new moment always did.

As I still lay in the hospital bed, I remembered how quiet

in Heaven it was at that change of moments. I thought to myself, "We do not know what quiet is." We believe that it is quiet, but it really is not. There is always sound around us.

Dampened Snow

I remember telling a person about that moment in Heaven when I was there and there was no sound. The person replied back to me, "Oh you mean like when I go up to the mountains in the snow, and all of a sudden it's real quiet." He was trying to get me to understand how sound is dampened or muffled by the snow. Even though snow itself may not make a sound we hear, there is still sound around that the snow is producing all the time. It may muffle the noise around, but the sound is still there. The quietness I am talking about in Heaven at that moment was not sound being dampened, there just was no sound at all.

God Is Moved

I found another verse in the Bible that speaks about being quiet before the Lord in Zechariah.

ZECHARIAH 2:11-13 (NKJV)

"Many nations shall be joined to the Lord in that day, and they shall become My people. And I will dwell in your midst. Then you will know that the Lord of hosts has sent Me to you. And the Lord will take possession of Judah as His inheritance in the Holy Land, and will again choose Jerusalem. Be silent, all flesh, before the Lord, for He is aroused from His holy habitation!"

God Is Being Aroused or Moved

This portion of scripture says that God is being aroused or moved to action. I came to understand that any time there was a new movement from God on this planet that there is silence in Heaven. I came to realize later that this silence was a sign of some great significant event that was going to impact the earth.

I believe that before any great movement on this planet takes place, it happens right after there is silence in Heaven. I believe the following events happened after silence in Heaven:

1. Abraham was being called by God (Genesis 12).

2. Moses was leading the Hebrew people out of Egypt and through the Red Sea (Exodus 14).

3. David was being anointed by Samuel to be king of Israel (1 Samuel 16).

4. Jesus was crucified on the cross (Mark 15).

5. The Holy Spirit came in like a mighty rushing wind (Acts 2).

I believe there are many, many more situations in the Bible in which silence took place before there was a great movement on this planet from God Almighty.

This silence that I experienced in Heaven was ushering in a change on earth that every born again Christian is a part of. I believe that we who are born again into the Kingdom of Heaven are destined to be a part of this great movement at this moment on earth. Are you doing your part?

PSALM 40:1-4 (NKJV)

I waited patiently for the Lord; And He inclined to me, And heard my cry. He also brought me up out of a horrible pit, Out of the miry clay, And set my feet upon a rock, And established my steps. He has put a new song in my mouth— Praise to our God; Many will see it and fear, And will trust in the Lord. Blessed is that man who makes the Lord his trust, And does not respect the proud, nor such as turn aside to lies.

CHAPTER 4

Worship Builds Fellowship with God and Others

Silence

I was giving praise to my Father with no sound. I came to understand that even silence in itself could be praise to God Almighty. It did not matter if I made a sound as long as I was praising my Father. The Holy Spirit, who lives inside me, was helping me to worship and praise God without a sound.

Lights of Heaven

Then, before the Throne of God an array of red lights, changing from light red to a deeper red, began to make bright circles within circles. This circle within circles went on for some moments and then changed to green lights. These green lights started to change from lightly green to a deep green. They did not make circles, but made rays that shot into the atmosphere and danced around each other. Again this went on for some moments. I cannot tell you how long these lights danced in silence, but I can tell you that these green lights then changed to blue lights. Here again, the blue lights went from lightly blue to deep blue. They moved like wavy lines up and down and all round. These blue lights danced for what seemed like a long moment also, and then changed into yellow lights. The yellow lights did the same things as the colored lights before, dancing in silence, but the shape of these yellow lights was as of small and large balls bouncing up and down. Then these yellow lights changed into orange lights. Orange lights became rolling movements like waves of water or dancing waves of water. After the change from orange lights, I saw another color that does not meet a description of any color I had seen on the earth. This changing of colors moved faster and faster as each change took place. Each change of colors had its moment to perform a dance before God Almighty who sits on the Throne. There were millions, upon millions, upon millions of these fast moving colors, each with its shape and performance before the Throne of God. The colors of these lights seemed to look like they were exploding within each other. The colors of lights were together, and yet they were very separated. I knew they were alive and brighter than any lights on earth. I knew that they, the colors of lights, were announcing the arrival of praise for God Almighty.

The anticipation from everyone there was growing stronger, because we knew that the colors of lights were announcing that praise was close. Praise was arriving for my Father, for my Lord and Savior, and for the Holy Spirit that lives in me. As the colors of lights moved faster and faster in changing from colors to different colors, I seemed to get more and more excited about what was about to take place.

Prostrated Before the Throne

I saw everything in creation that was already before the Throne of God on their hands, knees, and faces. They were lying on the holy ground in the direction of the Throne. Reclining on this blessed ground was their natural position when they were not actively praising God.

As I looked at each of them that were already before the Throne, I saw a light appear over one creation, almost like a spotlight singling out a person. This light was pure white, but it seemed to have something like lightning moving within it. The light had originated from God, and He had singled out this creation of His. This creation of His was some eloquent angel.

Beautiful Angel

All of a sudden I saw this beautiful creation of God, a creation of Life rising. This lovely angel reminded me of a beautiful, lovely lady. It was not a lady, but it reminded me of a very, very elegant lady. This angel was slender, almost like a pillar, a very tall pillar. This very tall, beautiful angel seemed to have around it a white light silhouette. Its hairs were light green and appeared to be as long as it was tall. Its hair also seemed to be dancing to a sound that I could not hear, and yet I knew there was no sound at that moment.

All at once, the colors of lights took on a rainbow shape as this angel moved from its knees to a full standing position. These beautiful lights made the form of a rainbow above its head! The colored lights looked like heat waves as they took on the form of the rainbow, and yet there was no heat. The angel moved to a standing position very, very, very slowly. How slow? I could not say for the movement seemed slower than any time on earth.

As this angel finished rising from its hands and knees and took a full standing position, this magnificent creation of God stood for a moment in silence. I looked at this angel, and it was much taller than all the other creations of God that I had encountered in Heaven, but before the Throne of God, this being was tiny in size. This angel stood with a greatness of life as it looked at God. Then, underneath this angel, the ground started to rise.

The holy ground, the glorified ground, rose up until it became a mountain. The beautiful angel of God stood on top of this newly found mountain. There appeared to be no distance between this angel and me. Because I was connected to this creation of life through Jesus and my Father and the Holy Spirit, I knew what its purpose was.

Extended Arms and Hands

The colors seemed to brighten up as this angel extended its two arms. Its arms were long and slender and moved with grace as it raised them into the atmosphere toward the Throne. At the end of each arm was a beautiful hand. I saw the hands unfolding from a fist-LIKE position. The palms were facing toward God Almighty. The hands seemed to be offering something to my Father. As the arms finished extending and the fingers on the hands stopped opening, I knew the angel was offering a praise of life to God Almighty. As this angel of God stood with arms and fingers extended, life came from its hands to the very tips of its fingers to offer itself to its Creator in praise. Even the hands that were facing my Father seemed to show each finger electrified!

Now that this creation of God stood in such a visible position, I could see the colors of this amazing, beautiful angel. It looked like light blue colors, shining through silhouettes of white lights. It was something like the blueness of the ocean on a bright day or like a lightly blue, blue sky on a cloudless day on earth.

Garment of Praise

This angel of God was wearing something that seemed like a garment. I knew it was like no clothing I had seen or experienced before. I knew God Almighty was shining out of this angel, and He was the garment. The apparel that this life creation was wearing looked like blue liquid lights. It looked like water flowing down from this angel's head to its feet. Each movement of the garment produced a brilliant bluish color.

Still, there was no noise even as this angel rose in such a great eloquent way. It seemed like a wind was blowing the garment. The wind was without a sound, and yet I felt no breeze at all. I knew that this garment which was created by God was a pure blue light that covered the whole angel of God, from the top of its head to the bottom of its feet. This blue garment even reached to the extent of the arms and hands. I was so excited to see everything about this great, beautiful angel of God. I knew that what I was looking at had been created out of pure Godly light, the garment of praise.

In the Hospital

As I thought about that moment when I was recovering in my hospital room, I would feel like my stomach wanted to burst out in praise to God. There was such a tingling in my fingers that I have no way to describe it to any human being on this earth. Even now, I hold onto those moments of holiness when I think about this angel in Heaven; and what I smelled, what I saw, what I experienced, and what I felt. Even when I sing praise songs to the Lord, I remember that moment of seeing how Heaven ushers in praise for God Almighty. When I sing to my God, there are still feelings that seem as if they will explode on the inside. These feelings cry out to me why I exist. They tell me I am created to give God Almighty praise with my whole being, body, and life in a real place of glory and holiness.

I even remember my eyes seemed to have a light of praise coming out of them. I am at a loss for words to describe the full moment of being there when this angel of life was ushering in praise for God Almighty. All I can say is that I wish that all of us who are born again would know or experience that moment of ushering in praise for God.

The only ones that praises are ushered in for are my Father and my Lord and Savior, King Jesus. There is nothing else in Heaven that deserves to receive that type of recognition.

Forty-nine Birthday Celebrations

I remember when my family wanted to celebrate my birthday on June 1st, sixteen days after I came home from the hospital. My wife was planning a huge celebration for me. She had invited friends from my job, church, and neighborhood. I don't remember how many she had invited, but it was a lot of people. I remember when she told me, and I remember how much I did not want to celebrate my birthday. She and the others wanted to celebrate it, because I was still alive on this planet. I understood that, but I still did not want to celebrate my birthday because of where I had been. There, the only one who received praise is my Father and Jesus Christ, no one else. I did not want to receive praise from anyone or about anything. I did not want anyone coming and celebrating or congratulating me. I had been in the place where the only one that received praise was God.

So, I started praying to God the Father about this birthday celebration. I was telling Him how I did not want to be honored because it wasn't me that deserved praise, but it was Him that did everything. As far as I was concerned, I deserved no celebration or praise at all. He knew from my heart that I was going to tell my wife to cancel the whole party for my birthday. And then I heard my Father God say to me through the Holy Spirit, "Celebrate it because you exist to have a relationship with Me forever." I remember the great joy that exploded on the inside of me and how grateful I was that I did exist. The greatest gift I had was to live with my Father, having Jesus Christ as my Lord and Savior, and having the Holy Spirit residing on the inside of me forever. Along with the privilege of celebrating with my brothers and sisters in the Lord forever, I could rejoice that I was born to fellowship with God Almighty forever. I can praise God for that. I could praise Him that I was born to have fellowship with Him forever along with His other offspring.

We did have a grand celebration on June 1, 2006. Most of the people who attended were celebrating my life back on this planet, but as for me, I was celebrating my fellowship with God Almighty forever.

I believe with everything that I am made up of, that every human being that is born on this planet, is born here so that they can have fellowship with God Almighty forever if they choose to.

PSALM 117:1-2 (NKJV)

Praise the Lord, all you Gentiles! Laud Him, all you peoples!
For His merciful kindness is great toward us, And the truth of
the Lord endures forever. Praise the Lord!

CHAPTER 5

Worship Calls Us to Praise God

Giving Always Praise

As I watched this beautiful angel of God extend its arms and open its hands, I saw something leave its hands. I know that whatever left the hands of the angel had something do with praise. I am not sure how to really describe how it looked. The closest I can come is that it looked like golden stars. I do know this. I felt a warm, calm air that seemed to enter my being and reach the very core of my essence. This feeling took place when praise left the angel's hands. I knew that this angel was giving away praise to God Almighty. I knew how I felt when the angel gave praise to God. I felt like I was part of the praise that this angel gave to my Father.

It was as if this angel of God was offering me up in praise, and I enjoyed the gift I had become to my Father. This angel was giving every creation of God in Heaven to Him, in praise. We were living worship in every sense of the word! At that moment, I knew I was fulfilling the call of my very existence. As I was fulfilling my life's calling, my connection to every creation of God became real to me. It did not matter where that creation was. The connection came about through worship and praise with everything in Heaven and on the earth.

In the Hospital

Back in my hospital room, I can remember thinking that all of God's creations are connected. We who have confessed with our mouths and believed in our hearts that God raised Jesus from the dead, as in Romans 10:8-13; we are connected. We are the branches that are attached to the Vine, Jesus, as in John 15:5-8; we are connected. We who are born again as in John 3:3; we are connected. We who are a new creation in Christ Jesus, as in 2 Corinthians 5:17; we are connected. And I knew that!

As I thought more on this praise that was leaving the angel's hands, I thought to myself that I had never seen praising God like this before. I now understood what it meant that we must worship Him in spirit and in truth. Every time we come to the point of worshipping and praising our Father from our spirit, we enter into His truth that presented our being to Him in praise. What we are giving away in praise is ourselves.

Singing Angel

Now as I was in Heaven, I saw this angel looking upward at God Almighty. It seemed to be focusing and looking into the very heart of His eyes. God Himself focused His eyes on this angel and smiled the biggest smile I've ever seen. I could see that He was very, very pleased with this angel of His. Then God gave some sign to this angel to start to sing.

What took place next with this Angel of God, this creation of God, I would not have ever thought of before if I had not experienced it myself in Heaven.

Silence came to an end when this angel opened its mouth. The silence was over with great joy. There seemed to be a smile in the atmosphere. I smiled, and every living thing around me was smiling a new smile, a smile we had never smiled before.

Sound of Pure Light, Thought, and Love

As the angel opened its month, a new sound came out, a sound that never before had been heard. This single sound was a beautiful sound, a great sound, a lovely sound, a surrounding sound, a sound of life. I can remember hearing the sound as it approached me and passed by me. It moved faster than the light that was moving around me. It was like a sound, and yet, it was like a light. The musical sound was made up of light and sound, sound and light. All I know is that it moved a lot faster than anything I could describe. Yes, it seemed like it was sound—light. It was music, real music, and life-giving music, this sound-light. It was a musical sound that I had never heard before, and yet, I understood the notes that this music made. As the sound passed by, all of a sudden, I understood it had a purpose. This musical sound of light was created for a purpose, and it was going to complete its goal.

Within a moment, another sound came out of this angel's mouth. Again, it was a musical sound of light with a purpose. It passed by me as I was still on my knees. The second sound went by a little faster than the first sound of light. As the second sound passed by, I, all of a sudden, understood it was pure thought. These sounds of light were not just sounds or music. They were sounds of pure light, pure thought, and pure love.

Then another sound of light and thought came out of the angel's mouth, and another, and another, and another, and another. They were becoming faster and faster and faster and faster. As soon as I heard them, ten more were coming. Then 20 more, then 100 more, then 50,000 more, then 1,000,000 more and so on and so on. The number of sounds of light and thought kept on increasing. The number of sounds of light and thoughts coming out of this angel was not countable, and no one was counting them. We were just accepting these sound gifts of light, thought, and love. Each musical sound had a purpose for us.

God's Love Sound

Then all at once, one of the musical sounds of lights and thoughts did not pass me by, but it entered into me. This sound, this sound of light, this sound of thought, this sound of love, penetrated into me. I knew at that moment that this music was not only light, thought, and love; but it was the musical sound of God's love made just for me. This sound of love entered into the very central nature of my being, into the heart of who I am. It joined itself with the Spirit of Holiness who resided on the inside of me. It joined itself to Jesus who exists within me. This sound of love created for me joined itself back to the Creator of Life who will always live within me.

Deep Calling to Deep

The musical sound seemed to integrate into my system and spread to every portion of who I was and was created to be. This musical sound of light, thought, and love caused me to want even more to tell my Father how much I loved Him. This movement within me was so personal. It was like deep calling to deep and sound calling to sound. It was my very pure spirit being called to the Creator of Spirits, my true Father.

My Sound of Life

All at once a sound that could not be created by me came into existence within me. God Almighty Himself could only spark this sound. It was my sound of life, thought, and love giving praise to my God Almighty. I knew my sound came into existence because of the invitation that came from within the angel of God.

As it grew within me, it brought a joy that had no end. It brought life that expanded within me. It brought truth and real rest. I was fed with this sound of music that is pure light, life, thought, and love. The sound that entered into me from the angel and the musical sound that came from within me became one musical sound. It was a sound of His light and my light, His life and my life, His thoughts and my thoughts, His love and my love. It was no longer two sounds, but one sound.

Personal Sound

I understood at that moment that this angel of God was being used to create a sound of praise for every creation of God in Heaven. There was no stopping of that musical sound that was personally created for me from reaching and completing its real purpose. This beautiful Creation of Life stood higher than any other being I had ever seen in Heaven. This blue-LIKE being with a watery-LIKE garment, long hair, and outstretched arms and hands was calling all of Heaven to praise.

Being Made to Worship and Praise

The musical sounds of light, thought, and love that were coming out of this being's mouth were a personal invitation to everything that was alive in Heaven to come to the Throne of God and give God Almighty praise. I knew this angel had been created for this purpose of calling all of life in Heaven to the Throne to worship God. I can remember that when I was called, I had experienced the purity of being made to worship and praise God Almighty for eternity. The joy of knowing this surpassed any pleasure I had before this knowledge. I chose with a pure heart to offer up praise with everything I was created of and was set up to be. I knew that He, God Almighty, would accept with great joy my offering of praise and worship. My praise came out of every bit of substance that I am. Every part of me was perfectly put together to worship God Almighty. My tribute was made to fit within God. He had made me His blessing. The musical sound of light and pure thought was the invitation that came for me, and then came from me to praise God Almighty. It was the key to unlocking the deepest thoughts of light and praise within me.

At Church on Earth

Months later, back on this earth, I was having a hard time being in praise services. I can remember having to hold onto the back of the benches at church and gripping them tightly with my hands. I had to do this, because many times when I was in a praise service, I would feel that sound of praise working within me. The words of my praise song would explode on the inside of me when I heard them. Everything about me seemed to dance and shout with joy with every song sung. Many times I had tears streaming down my cheeks, because I understood what we were singing to my Father. I understood how real it was.

Every song produced in Heaven, I had lived. The words and I were together. We were a song, a good song, but the words individually brought life to me. I did not just believe the words I sang, I experienced those words. I was living within the very thoughts of the music and the lyrics of those songs of praise. I understood the words of the song, before they came out of my mouth, before I could hear a sound, before others would try to harmonize, because I was living and being the words. Before the words were a thought within me, before they were a sound formed, before musical sounds had joined to my thoughts, before I knew in my spirit that I could hold onto them, before my real brain waves could move into motion, before I had the sound of pure praise coming up from within my being, before my mouth could sing a sound of this love song, I had already sung the Love Song to my Father.

This sound of life, thought, and love was my praise to God Almighty, my Father, coming from my heart. I wanted to give it as a gift to my Father.

PSALM 100:1-5 (NKJV)

Make a joyful shout to the Lord, all you lands! Serve the Lord with gladness; Come before His presence with singing. Know that the Lord, He is God; It is He who has made us, and not we ourselves; We are His people and the sheep of His pasture. Enter into His gates with thanksgiving, And into His courts with praise. Be thankful to Him, and bless His name. For the Lord is good; His mercy is everlasting, And His truth endures to all generations.

CHAPTER 6

Worship Is Preparation to Praise God

Pre-Destiny Sound

The sounds of lights were still coming from this beautiful angel of God, this mighty angel. I was no longer watching the other sounds that were coming from this angel. They were the musical sounds of lights for all the other creations of God. These sounds of lights were all predestined to enter into other beings of God in Heaven. These sounds that kept passing me by would go to other children of my Father, the other creative beings, the animals, grasses, flowers, trees, water, mountains, the atmospheres, and even the different forms and structures of Heaven. Everything in Heaven had a sound of light, thought, and love made for it. The call was going out to every living creature to come to praise God. Everything in Heaven was being invited to gather around the Throne of God Almighty, and all of Heaven showed up. To see everything in one accord, moving to worship God in praise, brought me great joy.

Sweet Aroma of Consuming Sound

As all of this was taking place, I was sinking into the sound that had entered me. I had become so consumed by the musical sound, and it seemed as if the music was being absorbed by me. As I became the music, and the sound became me, I remember the feelings that continued to grow in me. It was a feeling of being completed in every area of my life. I even started to take on a different fragrance.

The sound that entered me had a beautiful aroma. Every sound of praise had a distinct smell that was within it. The fragrance that came with this lovely sound of light, thought, and love had a new pleasing aroma. It was a new fragrance in Heaven.

In the Hospital

I can remember, in the hospital room, how I was trying to describe this scent to myself. I first tried to relate it to the aroma of flowers, especially roses. I love the smell of roses, but it was not even close at all. Then I thought about the scents of other flowers or a bouquet of flowers, like a florist fragrance. That also did not come near what I smelled. Every aroma on earth that I could think of that pleased me fell way short of the delightful fragrance of God's created sound.

Sweet Aroma

As I was in Heaven, this smell of praise caused us all to smile. One of the reasons I smiled was because I was a sweet aroma to my Father. Every destination where the sound of light, thought, and love ended, took on a new fragrance, a new scent of praise. Not only did we have new sound coming into the atmosphere of praise. We also had a new smell coming into and from the skies of Heaven.

Moving Toward the Throne of God

As the scent and sound penetrated the inward and the outward of me, I started going toward the Throne. Everything that was life in Heaven was moving near the Throne of God. The sounds from the angel compelled us all to go to my Father's Throne.

Sounds of pure light, thought, and love were still passing me by as I approached the Throne. I came to a spot or space. I knew I was in my place. It seemed like as I came to my place everything else in Heaven was reaching its space or place before the Throne of God Almighty. We all put our faces to the holy ground before the Throne in worship. Every living thing laid itself face down before God in worship.

Knees to Prostrate

As I fell on my knees and placed myself face down, the joy I had in going down, cannot be put into words. I remember the motion of moving to my knees and from my knees to the point of my chest touching the ground. In that action, I felt like I was experiencing a different area of glory in God. I would not come up the same, as if I were being baptized into something new or different for me for that moment. Finally, I placed my face into my hands with a great anticipation of how much love I was going to receive from my Father. Then I took my hands from my face and extended my arms before me in a prostrated position with palms up. I knew my palms were to receive a gift of love and to give love in praise.

The Beat of Heaven

The last sound to come from the angel of God was for the beat of Heaven, the beat that had always been there up to the moment of silence. This sound that came from the angel seemed to cause another beat, a new rhythm of love. Before the beat started, I knew the beat. It was new, and yet it was already in me and in all of the creations of God. It had come with the sound of light, thought, and love.

End of the Call from the Angel of God

After the last sound, the angel of God stopped singing. No longer did sounds come out of its mouth. Even though the angel stopped singing, I could still hear those musical sounds of light, thought, and love. It was like my thoughts were embedded in the sounds from this angel. As I looked up, I saw this great creation of God starting to lower its hands and arms to its sides very slowly. It began to bend its knees even lower. It took back the position of having been on its knees, kneeling before the Throne of God. This angel that called all of Heaven to praise before the Throne of God was now praising God in silence. It was lying with the front of its body toward the ground before God Almighty. The ground that this angel of God was standing on, which had become a high mountain, deflated and returned back to its original shape before my eyes. Both were still in silence giving great praise to God. They were worshipping Him in their actions and their movements. They had fulfilled their purpose of calling all of Heaven, all of life in Heaven, to praise the Almighty, the Life Creator.

The new beat of Heaven was beating, and this angel was no longer calling Heaven to praise the Lord. We had all come before the Throne of God to worship Him!

In the Hospital

In my hospital room, I remembered this experience of being called to praise God, my Father. As I stated earlier, even now being back on this planet, whenever it is time for me to give honor in praise, I still experience the great anticipation of joining with others and worshipping Him. I close my eyes and see everything in the room coming together in unity to give our Father God praise. I hear the call and see some responding to the call. They are the ones who also looked forward to this time of praise. They enter in with such easiness, because they hear the call. As we open our mouths to produce a sound, I have seen the love that leaves us go to our Father.

Also because of this experience of seeing what goes into preparing for praise for God Almighty in Heaven, I have come to understand that the preparation is worship itself. Preparing to magnify God is very significant. I found out that God receives those times of getting ready to worship Him on earth in the same way I experienced it in Heaven. He honors that time of preparing as worship in itself. So when song leaders, worship teams, and Christian musical artists practice to do their best in leading others in praise and worship, God Almighty receives that time of preparation as love for Him. He, even in this process of making everything ready, is adding to it to make it a sweet aroma to Him, just like I experienced in Heaven. I found out that even the preparation brings great joy to Him. Every detail in itself is praise unto God Almighty.

I had looked at the moments of practicing to praise as any ordinary time. I travel the world and see all types of praise for God. It seems like each one has a different way of preparing people to enter into worship and praise. The preparation or calling is as important as the actual standing before the Throne and giving our Father praise in song.

PSALM 122:1-9 (NKJV)

I was glad when they said to me, "Let us go into the house of the Lord." Our feet have been standing Within your gates, O Jerusalem! Jerusalem is built As a city that is compact together, Where the tribes go up, The tribes of the Lord, To the Testimony of Israel, To give thanks to the name of the Lord. For thrones are set there for judgment, The thrones of the house of David. Pray for the peace of Jerusalem: "May they prosper who love you. Peace be within your walls, Prosperity within your palaces." For the sake of my brethren and companions, I will now say, "Peace be within you." Because of the house of the Lord our God I will seek your good.

CHAPTER 7

Worship is the Voice of Praise

Connected

Now, as a new beat was called forth through the angel of God, this beat seemed to become greater every moment that I was in Heaven. Again everything was connected to it. Once the beat had started up and the beautiful angel of God had fulfilled its purpose, all I knew was that everything that made me a living being was vibrating and crying out now in praise to my mighty Father. My connection to everything in Heaven was still there, but it seemed like I was the only one getting ready to worship God. I knew; however, that all of Heaven was preparing to praise the Creator. We, every living being and every living creation, came willingly to praise the Lord with everything we had.

Great Multitude Praising God

Then it happened. I sensed to my right a great multitude of the creations of God. I looked to the right of me, and a great number of God's creation came out of their prostrated position and stood up on their feet. Others, like trees, just rose up to a vertical position along with all plant-LIKE creations formed by God. Mountains rolled up to a higher position as if they were being pushed up from the ground. Animal-LIKE creatures stood up on all four of their feet. Now everything that made this great multitude to my right, rose up to sing praises to God Almighty. Oh, how beautiful it looked to me to see them rise in unison!

Everything there that could lift something, lifted it up to God Almighty. I saw arms and hands extended toward God and branches from trees and other plants outstretched with immense joy toward God. Wings pointed in reverence toward Him, and the mighty mountain peaks of Heaven looked as if they were looking to their mighty God. Every living creation stretched toward God Almighty.

Joy

The joy that was already expressed in the life of Heaven was now coming off of this great multitude standing before God. They were all moving from His glory to more of His glory. His glory was consuming us, and we were consuming it. It ran through me like fire burning, and yet at the same moment, it also felt like life-giving blood going through me. I felt this life pumping from my essence throughout my entire being. It was pounding with a burning fire of His magnificent glory, and I knew whatever this glory was, I was becoming it.

His Eyes Were My Eyes

All I saw through my eyes is what He, my Father, saw through His eyes. I saw His glory, our praise, and worship, all coming together inside us, His creation in Heaven. As it came together,

I remember experiencing a power that was accelerating and was building up to a point where it seemed like I was going to explode in praises. I had known that each one of us before the Throne of God was going through the same experience. We all were going through this event of becoming a part of His Holy Glory. We were all becoming His glory, but at the same moment, we were individuals. Each of His creation had to take on His Glory in their uniqueness and in their own way.

Music and a Voice Coming Out of Their Mouths

What happened next with this great multitude was so very pleasurable to watch. Everything that had a mouth opened it up, and a voice with music came out in some holy substance from each being that was a part of this great multitude to my right.

The sounds from their voices or words were different from each other. They were singing in love, and I knew it was their individual words of love that no other creation of God could produce. Each singer had their own way, through sound, of telling their God how much they loved Him. Now every word was accompanied with a musical sound.

This musical material that came out of their mouths along with their words looked to me LIKE notes. They were not notes, but they looked like notes in appearance. I describe them as like musical notes because of how they performed before me. I saw them dance up to God Almighty who was sitting on the Throne.

These notes sounded like harps, trumpets, flutes, bells, violins, guitars, pianos, and even other instruments that I had never heard before. There were sounds of drums that weren't the main beat, but were different drumbeats. All of these sounds were coming from that great multitude that had just stood up, to sing to God Almighty. They were praising Him with every sound you could imagine and more. Each sound was made in pure love for God, and each sound was done with pure joy for the Father, the Savior, and the Holy Spirit. They didn't have any instruments in their hands. These sounds were coming from their mouths as notes of praises. They could produce different instrument sounds by just changing the shape of their mouths. Each musical sound had with it words to make one great sound of love to God.

A Servant's Heart

The other thing that was amazing was that every sound out of their mouths did not clash with the sounds that were being made by others who were singing at the same moment. They were not harmonizing together. The sounds were not in sync with each other, but still they didn't clash. This form of coordination was higher in unity than anything I have ever experienced on earth. The songs of praise I heard were coming from real servants of God. The main source from which these songs of praise came from was a servant's heart. Every creation produced an individual sound of its own, but each sound did not have to compete with other musical sounds that were being offered up to God Almighty as praise. These note-LIKE sounds seemed to enhance each other or, better yet, serve each other. They appeared to fit together in service to God like individual pieces of a puzzle. They were complete by themselves in what they were created to do, but they were also a part of a bigger picture of praise given in sound, given in service, and given in life to God Almighty. Billions, upon billions, upon billions and so on and so on, were these beautiful sounds of LIKE-notes; so many different sounds, and yet so beautiful.

In the Hospital

I can remember being in the hospital thinking about those sounds of musical instruments coming out of the mouths of all those creations of God. In my thoughts, I couldn't remember any instruments as I knew instruments being among the multitude of creation there. I thought previous to this experience that at least there would be harps and trumpets in Heaven. I had read how John said he heard and saw harps in Heaven. He said he heard trumpets in Heaven, but I cannot tell anyone that I saw instruments there, at least not like instruments here on the planet. Later on, I read where God placed symbols and flutes inside of Lucifer.

EZEKIEL 28:13 (NKJV)

You were in Eden, the garden of God; Every precious stone was your covering: The sardius, topaz, and diamond, Beryl, onyx, and jasper, Sapphire, turquoise, and emerald with gold. The workmanship of your (Tabrets in the King James Version of the Bible) timbrels and pipes Was prepared for you on the day you were created.

Tabrets or Tambourines and Pipes

The word Tabrets translates into the word tambourine or drum in Hebrew. The word pipes translated, means groove, socket, hole, cavity, settings, like a flute in Hebrew.

So here I read in the Bible where God did create a being that literally could produce sounds like instrumental sounds from within. I heard those sounds, and boy, did I listen to those sounds!

Now I faced another issue. Why didn't I see an instrument

like John or did I not recognize it as a musical instrument from earth? Then I read Revelation 9:13-14.

REVELATION 9:13-14 (NKJV)

Then the sixth angel sounded: And I heard a voice from the four horns of the golden altar which is before God, saying to the sixth angel who had the trumpet, "Release the four angels who are bound at the great river Euphrates."

Now I found out that this word "horns" in the Greek and Hebrew could mean like animal horns or a cornet, which is a valued brass instrument resembling a trumpet in design. Logically, from an earthly point of view, this would be more like animal horns found in Exodus 30:2-3. But since I was there, I saw that these horns looked more like instruments, but, again, not like what I would call horns on earth. First, they were alive. These horns were intelligent and could think on their own. In Revelation 9:14, they give a command to an angel of God.

So as I pondered on this, I decided that I did see instruments in Heaven, but they were way outside of any musical instruments I had seen on earth.

I came to realize there were no instruments like I had known instruments on the planet. Everything there could make a sound like a musical instrument. I heard the sound of trumpets, horns, trombones, tubas, cornets, guitars, electric guitars, violins, banjos, cellos, violas, harps, drums, and all kinds of drums (bass drums, snare, cymbals, tambourine, congas, bongos, triangles, kettledrums and even more drums). The main beat was different than any of the sounds made by these drums. It was not like any other drum sound. There were sounds of organs, pianos, xylophones, saxophones, flutes, oboes, whistles, and all kinds of bells, loud sounds of bells and quiet sounds of bells. There were lots of bells. There were more sounds that I had never heard from any instruments on the planet, but I knew the sounds were the sounds of instruments. How did I know? Because there was no holding back on the different sounds that gave God praise! Every sound of praise in itself wanted to express its unique sound that makes it a sound. I knew I wanted to open up my mouth to produce those beautiful, awe-inspiring, and unique sounds; and that is just what I did when I was in Heaven.

We are all created to bring a sound to God the Father, which no one else can deliver. Each and every one of us was made to give our Creator a pure love song, built from a servant's heart. He created us to be able to love Him with a sound of natural love.

In Heaven, I found out, that every human being created has a unique voice to give God praise with! Each one of our voices has a special place made for it, inside of our God. I came to understand that pure worship is done to last forever. It is produced in love and originates from a servant's heart.

PSALM 98:4-6 (NKJV)

Shout joyfully to the Lord, all the earth; Break forth in song, rejoice, and sing praises. Sing to the Lord with the harp, With the harp and the sound of a psalm, With trumpets and the sound of a horn; Shout joyfully before the Lord, the King.

CHAPTER 8

Worship Is Personal

I Wanted to Praise Him

All of a sudden, it was my moment to praise God Almighty. I wanted to praise and worship Him who created me. I had been looking forward to this point, to sing to Him and to praise Him in song.

As I tried to put into words that moment of singing my love song of adoration, it reminded me of how personal my song was. I was in a place where everything was in agreement in showing pure love to our Creator. That unity enhanced my ability to sing a perfect love song to my Beloved Father.

I was among all of His creation in Heaven. I was connected to all of the heavenly life by the Life Giver. Because of this connection to Him, we were all able to sing along with each other in a very personal way with our individual love songs, love songs made by us for Him. We all wanted to serve our God Almighty in praise through worship. By doing this, we also provided love to each other and to all of life in Heaven.

Personal Song of Love

Here I was about to give Him praise, a personal song of love. I was so excited. It brought me exceptional delight in what I was about to do. I was going to tell my Father how much I loved Him. All the time that the angel of God was calling me to praise, I had been looking forward to that moment that I would glorify my Father.

Being produced in me was a song of love for Him. As this was taking place, I was moving into a more joyful moment, a happier moment. I was moving again from glory to glory. As the praise song developed in me, I was moving deeper into His glory. It was not that the moments before were not great. It was just that the next occasion of singing to my Father was making every second in Heaven even greater. It was like the moment I had been in before had not existed, because the moment I was about to enter into, was more remarkable. It was like I had been so alive before, but now I was about to access newer life. Things seemed to get better and better every moment in Heaven as I worshipped Him, my Father.

I knew this was happening because of each sound of pure praise that was coming out of me. As each love song and real love tributes came out of me, I was fulfilling my purpose in worshipping Him. I was complete in praising my Father along with all of His creations.

The Holy Spirit at Work

The Holy Spirit residing on the inside of me was enhancing the praise that was coming out of me. This great tribute that I was presenting to my Father in great zeal in a love song, joined with His passion; and I had the privilege to give it to Him. It was much more than any love song I had ever sung before. I had only one agenda with this song of devotion and that was to honor Him. I desired to honor Him as I had never honored my Father before. I wanted to sing to Him how much I welcomed His love for me. I knew in that worship of praise that He cherished me! I wanted my song to bring my Father great joy. It was my personal song of love to Him.

I was expressing my affection for Him in a song because I could. It did not matter who else could hear me give my gift to the Gift Giver. I received a gift from Him, a gift of love created by my Father for me. He also created me for His gift of love, and I knew it. I wanted to thank Him with my praise song.

My Voice

I understood my voice was a gift from Him. He gave me a voice to thank Him. He created my voice to rejoice in Him. My voice of love was made for my Father to hear me. What a gift! He would listen to me. I had received the pleasure of knowing that He is hearing me. My Father is hearing my love song made for Him. I was satisfied with the two of us. He was hearing me and knowing how much I loved Him.

Time to Stand

Now was the time to stand. As I started to rise to my feet and stand with my arms at my sides, my excitement grew as I moved inch by inch upward. As I moved to stand to my feet, I knew I was moving into a posture, a stance that had been appointed by God Almighty, for me to take on in worship. I then started to move my arms, lifting them from my sides, as I elevated them upward with my palms open. I knew I was going to give my praise to my Father as a gift. Standing with arms up and palms open heavenward, I knew I was ready to worship Him. This position was my gift to Him, my stance of praise to my Father at that chosen moment.

I was created for this moment with immense love from my Father. I was prepared for this place to be able to open my mouth and sing unto Him. I was made to give God everything within me, everything that made me everything I was about to become in song. The stance I took at that moment was to show Him my love.

Deep Within Me

Deep within me was a substance made to present to my Father in love. What it was, I have nothing on earth to compare it with. I just knew it was only for my God. From this inner part of my inner being was a sound of praise. The Holy Spirit on the inside of me helped me to make it, and it came rolling up out of my eternal body with great joy. Everything that it passed on the inside of me expressed extreme happiness.

It was as if this substance of praise was moving from the core of my spirit and passing the inner parts of me, on its way to its destiny. It seemed to give out life in a greater way. It was like this praise song on the inside of me had become my food in Heaven. As it passed each part of my inner being, on its way out of me, everything within me was cheering it on as it moved up through me.

This tribute ran through me for my Mighty Father, the One who created me, the One who loves me, the One who cares for me, and the One who had brought me there and would never let me go.

As this sound of pure love moved within me to a place to be launched, I experienced another expansion of excitement. As this praise song advanced upward, there seemed to be an eagerness from it and me to be presented to my Father Almighty.

My Mouth Open

As my mouth was opening, just the very motion of the opening of my mouth in worship, I was filled with pure joy and love. That movement of my upper lip separating from my bottom lip was worship. All of a sudden my tongue started to form sounds, and I was ready to send forth a love song, a song of true adoration, a song of praise, a song of me giving myself to my Father in worship. My mouth seemed like it had its joy, its vibration of gladness, and it trembled with pure joy. It did this as I was forming it to release my song of praise.

Just as this song of praise seemed to jump from my tongue in joy, another song was rising within me. It was following after the first. It was like the first song was pulling the next praise song out of me. My lips again had great joy in being a part of this new song. This tribute in song also launched itself in joy towards my Father.

These songs of praise that were produced in me seemed to become faster and faster as each left my mouth toward the Throne of God. The sounds of praise were coming from my tongue and my lips with such happiness. This joy was happening because I was able to tell Him how much I loved Him in song and sound. The gratitude towards my Mighty Father, I could now express in song and music.

In the Hospital

I can remember thinking about those sounds coming out of me as I lay in my hospital room. As I thought to myself about them, I kept thinking that I heard those sounds before. At first, I could not put a handle on what kind of sound was coming out of me. It would be years, before I would come close to figuring it out.

Native American Flute

As I was doing a conference in Oregon, I heard a sound of music that I needed to know more about. The sound was coming from a Native American who was playing the flute. At the time, I did not understand why the music had drawn me to it. I had not put two and two together when I heard it. I thought that maybe because of my Native American Heritage of Choctaw, Chickasaw, and Cherokee, and me seeing this part of my family in Heaven, that perhaps, this was the reason why I was attracted to the music coming from the flute.

Later on, a good friend of mine, Dennis Dickson, played for me a Native American flute. I melted into the sound. I said to myself, I wish I could learn how to play that flute. He went on to tell me how he purchased that flute. He said something that when I heard it, my spirit jumped on the inside of me. He said that you do not pick the flute, the flute picks you. I understood what he meant when I later tested out the flutes by playing them. He said one would stand out because of the sound it made, and it would seem like it was made just for me. After that experience with Pastor Dennis Dickson, I knew I had to learn how to play the Native American flute.

One day in Hannibal, Missouri, I was in a Native American Store and came across flutes. I decided I would buy one. As the storeowner, Mike, showed me flute after flute, I came across one that seemed to sound better than all the rest I had played. When I heard the sound it made, I knew it was for me. I bought it! The musical sound that came out of it was in the key of A. As I started to learn how to play the flute, it hit me that this is the sound. Yes, this Native American flute sound came very close to the sound I made in Heaven.

When I sang my praise song unto my Father in Heaven, it was like a Native American flute sound. And yet the musical sound I played with my flute here on the planet was still way short of the sound I made in Heaven.

My Individual Light Sounds

As I was in Heaven, the sounds I composed were so beautiful. They were my praise songs, my light sounds, and my very personal love thoughts to my Father. Nothing could stop my sounds from reaching Him. Nothing could stop my Father from hearing His child's love song.

It was a love song, flute-LIKE music coming out of me. I loved everything about the song that was coming out of me. I knew I was created to produce this love song of praise. I didn't want to stop. I wanted to keep singing these flute-LIKE musical sounds in tribute to my Father forever. I did not want to stop singing. All the sounds were pure love, pure joy, and pure happiness. I did not want to stop. I wanted to keep on going... on and on and on and on. Again all these sounds were pure joy, love, and happiness to my mighty Father.

Holy Spirit Work Within Me

I knew He was helping me to produce these sounds by His glory that was living in me. It was the Holy Spirit. God Himself engaged with my spirit, coming up with this perfect music and praises. These songs were an appreciation of truth and light that had no ending and had been placed perfectly inside me by my Father.

It was like the Holy Spirit along with my spirit had teamed up to create living praise to give to God Almighty. I knew the sound of music that was coming out of me was alive because of the Holy Spirit who lives on the inside of me. This teaming made a sound of praise, a song of praise that was eternal and would not fade away. I knew that these sounds were becoming a part of God. I knew that my Father would enhance the life of the sounds, and they would become an extension of Him.

New Songs, Dancing Songs

The songs of praise that I could give Him were becoming a new song every moment. No song was ever the same. Every praise sound was new. I did not have to think of something new to sing. I just knew what to sing, and every song I sang was new.

After the songs of praise were produced within me and would come rolling out of my most inner being, they went out with great joy. The songs in themselves seemed to be happy. The songs appeared to be one big sound, and yet they were distinctive sounds coming out of me. They were great, beautiful, marvelous, and outstanding sounds of praise to my Father, my Life Giving Father.

They seemed to dance upward toward Him. They appeared to dance together as a part of each other. And yet, again they also were separated from each other. I knew the dancing songs of sound were another way to praise God in movement. These sounds of dancing, joy, music, and praise were my gift of love to my Father.

Living Waters

As I looked at each sound that left me and was getting closer to my Father, suddenly I noticed the living waters before the Throne rising into the atmosphere. I saw these living waters rise, wrapping up around every sound of mine. Every praise song of mine, that contacted these waters, would become surrounded by them. The waters appeared to take the shape of flutes. Every praise sound of mine that was within these living water flutes came dancing out of one of the many holes. It was as if the living waters were now playing my praise songs as flute notes. The living waters joined with me in adding their love song of praise to mine. The waters were serving me in playing my song of praise. The sounds became pure in their dance movements.

As my praise songs advanced toward the Father's Throne, the dancing music was enhanced by the pureness of the water-LIKE flutes. They looked like flute notes, but I was seeing this living water interact with each sound that came from another beautiful creation of God or me. Each time this interaction took place, the living water seemed to embellish the sound it had just enhanced. I believe it had something to do with its motions. This encounter of seeing the water play the sounds has had an impact on me in praising my Father.

As I saw and experienced what the living water was doing, I became more excited to be a part of this great moment of praise for my God. To see and experience the joy of all of God's creation praising Him in their own unique way had caused me to be built up in worship.

As my sound of praise and my song of love advanced towards the Father, I sensed that the atmosphere was going to do something with my songs, and it did.

In the Hospital

Later in my hospital room, I remember thinking to myself how I saw the living waters before the Throne wrap themselves around what I sang in praise to God. The waters seemed to be taking the sound of music coming out of me and playing them like someone on earth would play the piano or the flute or any instrument that would have air forced through it to make a sound. It was marvelous to have seen this being accomplished over and over again. The waters are the same that John wrote about in the book of Revelation.

REVELATION 7:13-17 (NKJV)

Then one of the elders answered, saying to me, "Who are these arrayed in white robes, and where did they come from?" And I said to him, "Sir, you know." So he said to me, "These are the ones who come out of the great tribulation, and washed their robes and made them white in the blood of the Lamb. Therefore, they are before the throne of God, and serve Him day and night in His temple. And He who sits on the throne will dwell among them. They shall neither hunger anymore nor thirst anymore; the sun shall not strike them, nor any heat; for the Lamb who is in the midst of the throne will shepherd them and lead them to living fountains of waters. And God will wipe away every tear from their eyes."

Atmosphere and Colors

In Heaven, as the waters surrounded these songs of praise, instead of them just dancing out, the atmosphere would form into a whirlwind or a twister and come through the living water in a way to blow my song of praise through the water flute. Then it would lift these songs of praise even higher to the very Glory of my Father. The colors that were coming from my Father would dance down to meet my sounds of praise and my songs of praise.

These wonderful, beautiful, great colors would dance down from God Almighty and meet my songs as they continued to rise. They then would dance together for a moment. Their dancing together was worshipping God. How long this went on I cannot tell you. I just knew that I received great joy in watching it take place.

After the colors and my praise were done dancing together, the colors seemed to escort my praise songs, my original light sounds, and my very personal love thoughts to my Father in dance. I did not only present them to Him, but now all of Heaven was rejoicing in my praise for Him. We had all teamed up to give God Almighty our praise. This was what every sound that was coming out of me was doing... meeting an array of activity as the sounds of music advanced to my Father, to my Lord, to that One to which I belong. I am His offspring and made in His image. My sound of praise was coming out of my innermost being with the help of the Holy Spirit.

In the Hospital

As I was in the hospital room, I thought about how these sounds of praise, these songs of praise, were offered up to my Father. I saw my song of praise rising like smoke from a fire just as John wrote of in Revelation.

REVELATION 8:3-5 (NKJV)

Then another angel, having a golden censer, came and stood at the altar. He was given much incense, that he should offer it with the prayers of all the saints upon the golden altar which was before the throne. And the smoke of the incense, with the prayers of the saints, ascended before God from the angel's hand. Then the angel took the censer, filled it with fire from the altar, and threw it to the earth. And there were noises, thunderings, lightnings, and an earthquake.

I came to understand how personal worship is to God. We are told in the Bible to do everything as unto the Lord in Colossians 3:16-17.

COLOSSIANS 3:16-17 (NKJV)

Let the word of Christ dwell in you richly in all wisdom, teaching and admonishing one another in psalms and hymns and spiritual songs, singing with grace in your hearts to the Lord. And whatever you do in word or deed, do all in the name of the Lord Jesus, giving thanks to God the Father through Him.

Now I know that when King David wrote in the Psalms, praise, he was not writing it to us, but every song he wrote was personal for him to God, to his Father. We just have the grace to read them. Even when Jesus, Himself, gave His Father praise, His praise was personal just between the two of them.

Every song we sing to Him must be our own love song to our Father. I have been in worship services with others when we just sang songs, and I have been in other worship services when it seemed like most of us singing had taken the song personally. There is a big difference. If you want Jesus to show up, worship must be heartfelt and true.

PSALM 111:1-4 (NKJV)

Praise the Lord! I will praise the Lord with my whole heart, In the assembly of the upright and in the congregation. The works of the Lord are great, Studied by all who have pleasure in them. His work is honorable and glorious, And His righteousness endures forever. He has made His wonderful works to be remembered; The Lord is gracious and full of compassion.

CHAPTER 9

Worship Is Action

Honor with Motions

It was now my turn to bow before Him and give Him honor with my actions and with my gestures. I lowered my hands and arms to my sides slowly. It was like I was moving in slow motion. I then took my hands and brought them together as if praying to my Father. I was not praying, but that is how I wanted to honor Him with my hands. I then started to bow my head and experienced much reverence for Him, as I made that motion of lowering it in praise. I felt the movement of bowing my head in praising Him. I had the great satisfaction of knowing that my song of praise and my sound of music were received by my Creator, who had created love to receive my worship.

I knew it brought joy to my Father. All I could do was put a smile on my face. It was not just any smile. It was a smile of knowing I had brought joy to the One who made me glad. I knew from that moment that joy was and is a part of me. I could now rest in that joy forever because of the happiness I brought my Father.

As my head rested in that joy, I started to bend my knees. As I lowered myself to the ground before me, I felt the joy I now rested in grow, as I got closer to the ground. Again, it was like I was moving in slow motion. My knees touched the glory just above the ground. His glory was in and around everything in Heaven. The experience in bowing before my Father became greater as my knees became a part of the power of God. It seemed like the ground was proud to receive my knees as I connected to the greatness that was around it. I became a part of His glorious and holy ground.

Team of Praises

I now understood that I had caused a reaction by kneeling on the ground. The reaction was that the Holy Ground also took its place in honoring God with me. We both became a team of praise to God Almighty. This was the same way as it was with the water, atmosphere, and colors earlier. The ground seemed to be happy in playing its part in being there for me to kneel on it in praise.

Excellent Praise

I then laid my body face down on the ground, with my hands and arms stretched out before me, with palms facing upward to my Father, in a giving and receiving form. The glory that I experienced at that moment was like a waterfall of God's greatness all over me. All of a sudden it seemed like I was vibrating, vibrating with supreme power, a power that was at the very core of my being. That same power from within me was also outside of me. I knew that this power was genuine praise from me to my Father. I no longer was moving slowly.

Every time I moved my head, my eyes, or even my nose, that power flowed out of me. Everything about me was giving Him praise. I could not make a motion that did not produce significant praise for my Father. I was feeling every action, every movement of my being, and yet I was moving faster and faster in this power of Praise. I could not calculate every action that produced praise to God at that point. There seemed to be no ending or beginning to these holy acts of praise that were coming from me. It was a substance of praise that I had coming out of me in motion. As I made a move, it was as if I were created only to make shifts with my body in praise to Him. There was no imperfection in my action in praise. All that I was then and would become is linked to perfect praise for God, my Father! It seemed as though the Holy Spirit, God Himself inside of me, was the lubricant for my motions in praise. Praising Him with action was easy.

I knew then, when I opened my eyes, that they were sending praises. The very closing of my eyelids, from top to bottom, was praise to Him. My smile on my face was honoring my Father. I seemed to have more energy as I moved in worship and praise. I knew I was moving from His glory to more of His glory.

Again, every moment of praising in action, coming from me, could not be compared to the next praise I produced in motion. Every action of praise I created through me for God Almighty was great, but the next moment of praise was more significant. It was so much higher that it made the previous praise coming from me, no longer any thought in my mind. All I could do was think about how much I loved Him.

Perfect Praise

Even though my turn was over in standing to praise and worship my Father, I still wanted to honor Him more. I knew that I could only give out perfect praise to Him. All, in Heaven, could only give out perfect praise. Yet with no other words to express what I experienced, all I could say was I moved from perfection in praise to another fulfillment of praise.

As I looked to the left, other creations of life were praising Him. They praised Him with their voices and also with their movements. This included all of the creations, flowers, trees, grasses, rivers, great bodies of water, waterfalls, colors, atmosphere, anything, and everything you can think of. As they were moving in motion, they were praising Him. As I looked, I saw the grasses and flowers as they moved in praising God Almighty.

Each movement by every creation of God was a form of worship and praise to Him. It was not out of the ordinary to see everything that was alive and moving in such a manner giving praise to their Creator.

In the Hospital

When I was in my hospital room, I meditated about those moments in Heaven. I thought about the grasses and flowers of Heaven and how they resembled a picture in my head.

They reminded me of a grassy field with wild flowers all throughout it. The sky that day was partly cloudy with patches of pure blue. There was a slightly warm breeze coming from the south, blowing across it. The grass and flowers in this field would move in a manner as if they were waves of water coming across an ocean. As they moved in this motion, you could hear the wind blow across the field.

This memory of the field brought back to me the moments in Heaven when I watched the grasses and flowers praise God Almighty.

Again in my hospital room, I remembered this movement of praise. I thought about how I would see it from time to time in worship. A person or persons would be singing to God, but very few other people were singing with them. It was not their time to sing. Everyone else was supposed to be listening.

But there were other times when songs were sung, and I would see people raising their hands or clapping. Some people would stand or kneel. Others would rock back and forth or tap their foot on the floor. All of these movements and others are how people give God Almighty praise through action.

Now I know that even when we move our body in those times of worship, God Almighty sees it as another way of honoring and praising Him.

PSALM 145:3-7 (NKJV)

Great is the Lord, and greatly to be praised; And His greatness is unsearchable. One generation shall praise Your works to another, And shall declare Your mighty acts. I will meditate on the glorious splendor of Your majesty, And on Your wondrous works. Men shall speak of the might of Your awesome acts, And I will declare Your greatness. They shall utter the memory of Your great goodness, And shall sing of Your righteousness.

CHAPTER 10

Worship Comes from the Heavens

In the Hospital

I remember thinking to myself as I was in my hospital room, how beautiful it was for me to participate with all of God's creations in Heaven in praising God Almighty. We were all created to love our Creator, our Life Giver. How amazing it was! One of the most amazing creations I participated with in praising God was the very Heavens of Heaven.

Heavens of Heaven

As I was in Heaven, I looked at the atmosphere all around me. The colors were changing every moment as we all worshipped God in praise.

The sky in Heaven was a multiple of atmospheres. I could not tell you how many different creations of God made up the skies of Heaven. As I looked upon them, there were various forms, but they were all the Heavens of Heaven.

When I first entered into Heaven, the color of the atmosphere was a golden white. It looked like white in some areas with gold streaks throughout the sky. In some areas, the gold colors faded into the white areas. Some of the golden beams pointed away from God on the Throne. The rest of the beams pointed toward the Throne, in what looked like the shape of an arrowhead.

The atmospheres sometimes would take on the form of what looked like curtains waving in the wind. At other times they looked like a big white waterfall, but the water was moving from the surface of Heaven upward. Often I saw them move like water rolling over and over in the shape of a water wheel. I also experienced the skies forming what looked like water spouts, with the small ends up in the heavens and the large ends on the surface. There were more motions that I saw the atmospheres accomplish, but all of the different shapes of the sky above me brought great tranquility to every area they were suspended over.

I also watched the interaction of the colors from the Throne of God with the atmospheres. As I saw the colors coming from the Throne, the rainbow colors would reflect off the skies of Heaven. This reflection would cause reactions that expanded the skies of Heaven. I came to understand that God was still creating more heavens in Heaven. Each new color from God Almighty was life to the atmospheres of Heaven.

With this life came a new smell and taste that was imparted into the skies. Each creation of the heavens had its own sweet smell, and there is no natural scent on earth that compares. Also, the taste of the skies of Heaven was beyond any creation on earth. Each area, smell, and taste was a big part of the experience of the heavens of Heaven.

Heaven Moving to Worship

When that moment came about for the skies to get together at the Throne of God to worship and praise Him, the heavenly skies took on a different role than when I had first entered into Heaven. The colors that made it look so golden white now turned to a vibrant white. This white color stood out from all the other white colors in Heaven, but God's Glory around the Throne was still the whitest.

As I saw the colors changing, the smell and taste of Heaven also changed. For that occasion of worship, a newly created smell and taste of praise came into existence. All of this took place when the atmospheres received their call to praise and worship at the Throne of God Almighty, from His beautiful angel, which was a sound of pure light, pure thought, and pure love.

I remember the skies above the Holy ground moving toward the Throne. As they moved, it was like a big windstorm moving over the ocean. Everything that was in its path cheered it on. I knew, myself, that when they, the heavens, gathered themselves over me, I wanted to jump up and give praise to my Father for the brilliant skies, God's beautiful creation of atmospheres.

As these skies of Heaven came closer to the Throne, they were making joyful sounds. They sounded like great and loud thunder, but thunder unlike any thunder I could ever recall hearing before. It was like the sound of thunder coming through hollow pipes. The sound seemed like it was rolling around and around and around through hollow pipes. Each sound was booming like it was coming through a large, hollow metal tube.

Sound of Thunder

With each sound of thunder, there were other sounds of thunder following the sound I just heard. Every single moment of thunder had another sound of greater rumbling building on the previous sound of thunder. Embedded inside each thunder was a sound of joy that I have no words to explain. I just knew that the sounds were a passionate tone from the atmospheres about their Great Creator. It was as if the love and joy within the noise of thunder had a sense of peace passing understanding. These sounds of thunder or songs of thunder that were from the heavenly skies were louder and louder, as each thundering sound rolled out of the atmospheres. The heavens making this powerful music were in pure joy. The musical sounds themselves were a boom within a boom and another boom within a boom that was larger in sound than the previous increased sounds.

In the Hospital

When I was in my hospital room, I thought about those thundering sounds of joy! What they reminded me of was a great fireworks celebration, like the last finale of the show, where many rockets are shot up into the dark sky with explosives that would reach their destination and explode around the same time. I would see this type of show mostly at amusement parks or at a Fourth of July celebration in the United States. Another example is when I would be in a theater watching a movie, and many explosions would take place within a movie. I would hear the explosions from all points in the theater room because of the surround sound. I remember how it seemed like I should have melted with each explosion of joy expressed by the atmospheres. In Revelation 10, John writes about the atmosphere of Heaven.

REVELATION 10:1-4 (NKJV)

I saw still another mighty angel coming down from heaven, clothed with a cloud. And a rainbow was on his head, his face was like the sun, and his feet like pillars of fire. He had a little book open in his hand. And he set his right foot on the sea and his left foot on the land, and cried with a loud voice, as when a lion roars. When he cried out, seven thunders uttered their voices. Now when the seven thunders uttered their voices, I was about to write; but I heard a voice from heaven saying to me, "Seal up the things which the seven thunders uttered, and do not write them."

This chapter gives the best examples of what I experienced about the skies of Heaven. John called them the seven thunders. I saw them as multiple atmospheres.

Dancing Skies of Heaven

When I was in Heaven, I saw the skies of Heaven merge with some of the colors coming from my Father. I saw them look as if they were dancing together in worship in the atmospheres of Heaven. They would swirl up and down and around together.

Other colors that left the Father met up with the praise coming from all of the creation. They would join with the sounds of life and joy. These colors would then dance with them, as they had danced with my praise song. As they danced, the colors would escort the different songs of praise in dancing up to God Almighty.

The difference with the thundering sounds of praise and colors was that even the sounds of thunders merged with the colors. It was not just the atmospheres of Heaven that merged, but also the very essence of their thundering sounds. These two creations became one nature in movement. They moved as one being and not two separate creations of God. They were separated, but because of their willingness to join in praising God, they no longer showed evidence of that separation. They now became one in praising God. As the merging of the colors and thundering sounds took place, a new thunder would come forth and make a new sound of praise to God Almighty.

New Sounds of Thunder

There were sounds of thunder made out of the excitement the skies had in praising God Almighty. These thundering sounds of praise coming from the atmosphere would start to echo over and over and over again. Each booming had another sound within the booming. It was as if everything that made the sound was giving another explosive sound within each boom. Because of this, I would experience many roars of the immense joy of praise to my Father. It was like the skies in Heaven wanted each thundering sound of praise to produce a greater sound of thunder in praise to its Creator. I knew each sound was an eternal musical voice.

With all of the sounds of thunder, the atmosphere was moving in a dancing rhythm. They would make themselves into a ribbon or flag-LIKE shape throughout the heavenly sky with each boom.

In the Hospital

I remember being in my hospital room thinking about the atmospheres praising God and how they seemed to take on the movement of flags or ribbons blowing in the wind. They seemed to move like cattails waving in the wind on a windy day or as waves of water moved the bottom halves of the cattails and wind moved the top shafts. Sometimes the cattails would wrap themselves together. In this formation, it looked like they became one long cattail.

The Scenes of Heaven

In Heaven, this scene would play over and over each time a little different than the one before. The heavens would separate and move in different directions from each other for a moment and then back together. Sometimes they reminded me of swarms of birds darting in the sky together. They would, in one moment, dart to my left, and then shoot to my right with each thundering sound of praise to God.

In Heaven, I knew that each and every movement the atmospheres made was dancing in praise to God. I was experiencing the beauty of each movement of the skies in Heaven moving to the thundering sounds of praise to God Almighty. They would move in horizontal lines or they would go in vertical lines; all would move in circles while others would move into a half-circle; they might move in a zigzag motion or perhaps diagonal waves; they had more movements than I can even describe. All of these actions came with the sounds of thunder. Even though I was not dancing to the thundering sounds with my spiritual body at that moment, my inner being was dancing with every movement of the atmosphere.

In the Hospital

Back in the hospital room as I remembered the waves of atmosphere going up, down, and all around in praise to God, this praise of the atmosphere reminded me of seeing waves of heat rising from concrete. It was like the skies of Heaven were lifting themselves up in praise, like when I raise my hands in praise.

I saw the worship for my God, from the atmosphere in waves within waves, rising. Each thundering explosion of praise for God also caused others to praise Him. I came to know through the skies of Heaven worshipping and praising God that when I move the air around me in clapping or raising my hands, I am also causing it to give praise to my Father.

PSALMS 148:1-6 (NKJV)

Praise the Lord! Praise the Lord from the heavens; Praise Him in the heights! Praise Him, all His angels; Praise Him, all His hosts! Praise Him, sun and moon; Praise Him, all you stars of light! Praise Him, you heavens of heavens, And you waters above the heavens! Let them praise the name of the Lord, For He commanded and they were created. He also established them forever and ever; He made a decree which shall not pass away.

CHAPTER 11

Worship in Dance

A Multitude of All Kinds of God's Creations

Another group started to praise God Almighty along with the atmosphere, when I was in Heaven. This group was still in front of the Throne but was a little before me and above me, suspended in the skies of Heaven. How high above me, I cannot tell you. They seemed to be far overhead but very close at the same time.

This group was an immense multitude made up of all kinds of God's creations. Not only were there birds and other flying animals, but also things you would say couldn't fly. These creations of God consisted of grasses, flowers, trees, mountains, rivers, and many more beings. Of course, there were also many different kinds of angels and then there were the Redeemed. None of this group was flying. They stood on or in the skies as if they were standing on solid ground.

Small Sounds of Thunder

They were all dancing to the thundering sounds of praise and music in the heavens. As each creation made its dance move, this movement seemed to cause a lower impacting sound of thunder. As I watched the dancing, I saw how softer thundering sounds came into existence. When the louder thundering sounds came into contact with those who were dancing, the movement of the atmosphere around the dancer would cause a small sound of thunder. The motion of the moving bodies in praise dances caused ripples in the atmosphere. It was like rings of water created because of a rock that was thrown into a pool of water. Just like those rings of water, the waves moved outward, away from the dancer. When these ripples would come in contact with the loud thundering sounds, they both would produce a lower thundering sound. The bigger sounds of thunders were bouncing off the motion of the waves in the atmosphere, and a new sound of thunder was made to offer up in praise to God. Even though they were all doing their dance in a unique way, none of the action distracted from any motion of worship that was caused by a new thundering sound.

Flowers Dancing in Praise

One of the creations of God that stood out to me was the flowers of Heaven. They brought a smile to my face as I watched them dance in praise to God Almighty. As they praised God, I could see that there were so many different types of dancing flowers in Heaven. Some were small and very tiny. If they had been on earth, I probably would not have been able to see them. Others were very huge. They were bigger than any plant I had seen on Earth. And then, there were many kinds of flowers in between the tiniest and the largest. In Heaven, there seemed to be many more different types of flowers than I believe could be found on earth.

The number of twists and twirls they performed amazed me, and this twirling was their praise dancing. In seeing the flowers spinning and turning, they seemed to make themselves look like rotating rainbows in a field of wildflowers.

Not all the flowers were the same. The Creator uniquely made each flower. Each flower was formed to bring full beauty to an already beautiful place and now was giving that loveliness back to God Almighty in praise.

One of the ways they were doing this was by raising their stems of leaves as they danced before the Throne of God. To see them all raising their leaves in praise, twisting and twirling at the same moment, was amazing!

Another way the flowers intensified their dancing was through smell. Every flower in Heaven had a particular smell of praise that came off of it and out of it. I knew this smell amplified its praise and also enhanced its dance of love. Not only could I smell the fragrances, but it seemed as if I could taste them. The flowers showed me how everything in Heaven gave everything they were in praise to their God. It was so wonderful and beautiful to be a part of that reality of praise to my Father. I was in awe of being in such holiness.

In the Hospital

As I sat in my hospital room later thinking about those flowers dancing and praising God, their rotations reminded me of seeing helicopter blades turning at full speed. They also seemed to look like rainbow twisters dancing because of the trillions of colors that they were displaying.

The other thing that I admired about the flowers' dancing was how they praised together. They were so unified in their dancing with each other. They were so much in unison in dancing with the thundering of the atmosphere. They were so much in being of one accord with the love of all of God's creation.

This oneness in praise that I had experienced produced high energy and power. If it had been electricity, I guess it would have been able to light up every large city in the United States or even the world. I just knew that I had never seen power like that on earth.

I also recalled the joy that I saw coming from each flower as it presented itself to God Almighty in a beautiful dance. Some of them raised their leaves to enhance their beauty, while others moved their flower petals to form a shape that would give Him praise.

Still Pondering Flowers in Heaven Years Later

Months and years later, I am still pondering about those flowers in Heaven. They showed me pure praise with exceeding joy through their smell. They had opened up a whole new understanding for how we honor God. This smell from the flowers showed me how everything in Heaven celebrated God Almighty in two different ways.

One way we celebrated Him was outwardly, and the other was inwardly. Those flowers of Heaven helped me to give and show honor to my Father in an entirely different way than I had ever done before. I did not know we could express our love toward Him from within and from without.

The smell of the flowers in dancing also helped me to come to a greater understanding of this pure praise. The pureness of producing an outward and an inward praise comes from a truly loving essence that is created by us for only the Creator. The flowers had that sweet aroma that was made only for God.

It was perfect coming off and out of them. Because of this encounter with those flowers of Heaven, I saw how we who are born again could and should always praise God from within and without. I experienced all of God's creation there that did just that! All in Heaven had beautiful outward worship and a joyful inward praise to offer Him who sits on the Throne.

I remembered that as the flowers produced the praise as they danced before the Throne, I could see honor leave them and go towards God. At the same moment I would know that glorification of God was moving deeper within them.

We all in Heaven could see the outward expressions of praise. We even saw how other creations of God reacted to that form of love. I clarified that type of celebration earlier when I explained what it was like for me to sing praises to my Father. I knew the process of producing this outward worship was the same for all in Heaven. We all gave different outer thanks to God with love. The flowers did it with their dancing. I could see and feel the outward praise that was leaving them and advancing toward the Throne. I saw an external vibration of love move away from each flower directed to the Throne of God.

The inward devotion is much harder to explain, because it is not what I saw, but what I felt. Now I felt the love and worship from the flowers as I watched their dances and smelled their fragrances.

Their inward expression started at the same point where the outward appearance of worship started but moved in the opposite direction.

Praise for God is produced in all of us with the help of the Spirit of Holiness, as I stated earlier. This area is in all of God's creations that are connected to Him. It is eternal—an area that time does not exist in. For the redeemed, it comes about when we are born again, reconnected back to God. This was one of the many things that was lost in that first sin of humankind (Genesis 3). It has been restored because of Jesus dying and being raised from the dead (Ephesians 2). Now every human on earth has the opportunity to receive this eternity existing on the inside of them forever by accepting Jesus Christ as Lord and Savior. This area resides on the inside of every born again spirit, where God exists on the inside of us that are saved from death. Our true praise for God is produced in this area with the help of the Holy Spirit. This is why we can create worship in Spirit and Truth (John 4).

So I felt that the expression of love for God Almighty moved on the inside of the flowers in this eternal realm. I felt it inside of me when I sang praise to God in Heaven. This praise on the inside of the flowers expanded in this realm. If I say it moved deeper in, I am way short in describing what took place. All I know is that it never ends in both directions, outward or inward. Our worship and praise has no end to it. I sense that all of God's creation in Heaven went through this systematic process of inward devotion towards God. I also felt that we, who were the redeemed in Heaven, had our faithful love partner with the Holy Spirit that lived in us.

Because of experiencing this outward and inner worship, I changed my approach to praising my Father. Even now when we worship God through praise and adoration, we are actually sending Him a substance that is in eternity from two different directions. Every person that is redeemed, born again, or a new creation in Christ does that when they give praise to their Father. They provide an outward and inward celebration that is in eternity, whether they realize it or not.

Other Creations of God Dancing

In Heaven, not only were the flowers dancing, but also other creations of God were a part of this significant number who were in the heavens dancing. Each being danced with joy, each creature danced with grace, and each creation danced with pure love. There were so many different creations dancing before the Throne. There were grasses, flowers, bushes, trees, valleys, hills, mountains, rivers, lakes, seas, colors, fires, lights, atmospheres, stars, seraphs, cherubim, archangels, fishes, birds, animals of all kinds, and the children of God. Everything God had created at some moment danced in praise to Him. Some danced in the skies of Heaven, while others danced on the holy ground in Heaven.

As I saw the many different living beings of God dancing before Him, I was amazed. It was an incredible situation to be able to see the many unique movements that were used to praise God. Many of these different dance moves fascinated me because of the creations that were performing them.

Grasses Dancing in Praise

I watched the grasses of Heaven do their dancing before the Throne. Just like the flowers, they came in all sizes and colors. They did some running and jumping moves in rhythm with the thundering sounds of joy. They looked to me like they were running in circles and going around and around and around. Once in a while, they would jump. It was no little hop, but a great leap of joy. The grass would make running circles in one direction, then stop, turn around, and head in the opposite direction. Now those running around were not one or two circles, or even 500 circles, but millions upon millions upon millions of circles. They were not all going in the same direction. They were like running in all directions at the same moment. Some were horizontal and some were vertical circles; some were half-horizontal and half-vertical circles; a number were a quarter of the way horizontal and vertical circles; others were big circles or small circles. I cannot tell you how many times they came together to form one big loop to dance, but I did know that when this happened among the grasses of Heaven, it was no small offering of love from them. One thing I also knew was that they, the grasses, really did enjoy dancing before the Throne. They enjoyed dancing in praise to their Creator with vast love for Him.

Trees Dancing in Praise

The trees of Heaven were one of the first creations of God that danced before Him. These trees would wave backwards and forwards to the songs of praise and to the thundering sounds of love. Just like the grasses, they moved in rhythm together. As I saw them bow before the Throne in dance, I became intrigued as to how they lowered themselves in praise to God Almighty. I saw the trees bend over and over and over. They were not on the ground when accomplishing this dance move. They were still suspended in the heavens as they bent over to the holy ground.

As they started to bend from their midsection over, none of them seemed to move fast or slow. I had nothing to measure the speed at which they moved, but it was just a wonder how they danced as they did.

I would always know which tree or trees were going to make the next move of bowing. I would first see the very tippy top of the tree make a slight move, like someone tipping their hat in respect to another person. Just as I saw that tipping at the very top of the tree, the tree would start moving in the direction of the Throne. The middle of the tree would start to bend, and it would keep bending until it touched the ground of Heaven.

Sometimes as a tree would come close to touching the ground, the holy ground would create a hole as if it were opening up to swallow the top of the tree. I understood the ground was dancing with the trees in praise when it did that. This opening and closing of the ground was its way of dancing with the trees. Once the tree or trees had finished in bowing in praise to God, they rose back up to their full height and were even a bit taller.

Again just like the grasses and flowers, the trees came in all different shapes, sizes, and colors. As I watched all these different trees worship God in praise, I understood that all creation around the Throne came only to give their fullness to God in praise.

I kept looking up at the trees in the atmosphere dancing. It seemed like there were more trees in the skies of Heaven dancing every moment. It was like trees were calling to other trees on the divine ground to join them in the skies, and they were coming. Tree after tree was becoming a part of the great tree dance in praise to their Creator.

Mountains Dance in Praise

As I was experiencing in Heaven the flowers, grasses, and trees dancing in praise to God Almighty, there were still other creations dancing. The mountains of Heaven were one of those creations. The magnificent mountains of Heaven also danced to their Creator.

When I first saw the mountains answer the call to praise from the beautiful angel of God, they resembled mountains on earth, but with greater majesty and wonder about them. At the very top of each mountain was a white light. These lights of white were not snow. I have not yet found a way to explain that brightness to my satisfaction. To say it is like snow is inadequate. That blazing white substance on those mountains in Heaven had something to do with Jesus' glory. It was different than anything I knew about or heard about His glory before, but I just knew.

The mountains moved, as in worship, like waves coming off the ocean. They rolled like the sea waves on earth, side by side. I saw one row of mountains pass me by and then another came right after. How many rows of individual mountains came to the Throne to praise Him? All I can say is that the number of them would surpass the number of mountains that exist on our planet. It was a huge number of God's creative mountains.

Now when the mountains first showed up, they were all on the holy ground, but I saw them rise into the skies of Heaven. They ascended into the skies as they approached the Throne.

First it seemed like the mountains could step up into the skies of Heaven like they were stepping on stairs. The atmospheres of Heaven formed themselves into stairs, and it looked like the mountains hopped or jumped from one level to the next step until they reached their station in the skies of Heaven. I knew the mountains did not need the atmospheres to help them reach their spot for dancing. I knew that out of servanthood the skies of Heaven became stairs to enhance the mountains' dance of praise. Also, they were dancing with the mountains of Heaven in making the steps. They, the atmosphere and the mountains, produced a new dance of praise to their Creator.

The second way the mountains became a part of the dancing in the heavens was that God just lifted some of them up. He just willed it, and it was done! When He picked them up with His will, it was like one moment they were on the ground and the next moment they were in the skies. It was fast! Even though I was in Heaven, it was so fast that I did not and could not see it. The speed of the move was outside of my comprehension, even in Heaven. All I knew was God Almighty placed them in the atmosphere to dance before Him.

Once a mountain of Heaven took its place to dance, it did. The movement of the mountains was something to watch. Many of them just quaked in place. Others moved around together with some of the many creations of God and even the Redeemed. They seemed to enjoy dancing with and to the thunder.

To truly try to describe their movement is difficult to put into human words. I did see them dance in love, joy, and a peace that passed all understanding. That moment of seeing these great majestic wonders of Heaven giving their fullness of praise in dancing to God Almighty was so incredible. I knew by watching them that they loved their God Almighty with everything they had.

The Redeemed Dancing in Praise

In watching this dancing that was taking place in the heavenly skies above me, I saw those in God's creation that seemed to take on dancing with grace. They were the redeemed, the children of God, those who were born again, and those who truly were the offspring of the Father. They had become God's perfect creation and were being lifted up by the very sounds of praise into the atmosphere in Heaven.

To see the sounds of praise raise a child of God up was like seeing a feather floating upward before your very eyes. As I watched each dancing offspring of the Almighty rise into the skies of Heaven, everything I was made of wanted to be a part of that great dance of praise. I knew I was redeemed and wanted to share that joy with my Father in dance. We that were made in His image had an unspeakable joy that we wanted to show Him in dance.

As God's children took their place in the Heavens of Heaven, they became a significant number. I knew deep down inside of me that the Redeemed had been waiting for their moment to praise their Father in dance. I just knew that they were created for this occasion to dance to the One who crafted them out of love that exists forever. Now all that waiting was over, and in a moment they would dance for Him, their true Father, out of pure grace into undiluted love.

The significance of seeing the Redeemed, God's children, dancing was an all-absorbing moment in Heaven for me, because of my connection to the Redeemed through the Holy Spirit that lived on the inside of me. I now know this connection started here on earth with some of the Redeemed who were dancing. I was now with them in Heaven watching them dance in praise to our Father. I was aware that we had had this shared experience of living on earth and were connected. One of them that I was connected to was my grandmother, Mary. I not only watched her dance, but it seemed like every move she made, I made. I experienced her dance for God because of our connection.

The dance moves of praise done by the redeemed could not be performed by any other creation of our Father. Only we, His children, could dance the dance of the Redeemed. The same was with songs that we sang. We sang a song that only the Redeemed could sing. Never could another creation of God dance like the Redeemed. The flowers, grasses, trees, mountains, skies or any other beings of God could not dance as the Redeemed, His offspring. Only those who were born again, only those who confess with their mouths and believe in their hearts, only those who were new creations in Jesus, they were the only ones who could dance the dance of the

Redeemed, His children.

They were dancing with the powerful colors that were coming from the Throne. Those beautiful colors were moving around them and streaming behind them as if they were riding through the wind. The colors, by dancing with the Almighty's offspring, were celebrating life, the life of God within His children. I knew all of this was because of what my Lord Jesus had done.

My Turn to Dance

Now it became my turn to stand up to meet the others in the sky to dance. I started to lift off the ground and into the atmosphere of Heaven. I, too, was being carried upward by the sounds of praise coming from the music of the skies, the voices of honor coming from the children of God, and the music crafted by the precious creations of God.

As I took my place, I started to dance with the atmospheres, trees, grasses, mountains, flowers, and much, much, much more. I danced in celebration to my Father because of what Jesus had done. Everything about me wanted to dance. I seemed just to vibrate with love and joy for my Father. There were no words on earth created to give even a close description of how I danced in praise. My dance style was very multifaceted in itself. I did not want to stop. I, a creation of God and a child of the Almighty, had every reason to dance in praise to my Creator.

Avenues of Love

We that were redeemed could and did dance in praise to our Father with everything that lives in Heaven. We did it with great joy. God's children danced before Him, like little children would dance before their parents. Every child of God in Heaven had perfect rhythm and a beat that is out of time.

The celebration continued in Heaven in song, in dancing, and in ways I cannot describe. None of these different forms of praise interfered with each other. Each one of the styles of praise had its own uniquely made avenue to reach my Father in love.

In the Hospital

As I thought about the praise dancing when I was recovering in the hospital room, all I could say to myself was, "Praise God!" I remember seeing the dancing in all of its different forms connect to God Almighty. Each action, each gesture, and each motion was a perfect praise to be a present to Him, our Creator. I thought, "What a great honor to be a part of this type of love to God."

I noticed how each dance was so independently done, yet none interfered with others while being presented to God personally. He received them all in an individual way as if that being was the only one dancing before Him, and He loved it.

Dancing or giving movement in praise had not just started at that moment but was already going on when I entered into Heaven. It was not being performed in the same magnitude as when we did to praise God at the Throne, but there were always those who were dancing in glory to God, just like there are those who are singing before God always. The intensity of the dancing started when that first song of praise went up from us, His creation.

I remembered, as I meditated, how the dancing did not stop before the Throne, except when all of Heaven became silent. There was no more dancing during that moment.

Because of this experience, I came to understand that movement in praise or dancing has always been a way to worship God. I also understood that it always would be a part of the celebration in Heaven.

I thought about the movement in Isaiah 6:1-4. The angel's very movements were thanks to God Almighty. To me, it seemed as if they were dancing.

ISAIAH 6:1-4 (NKJV)

In the year that King Uzziah died, I saw the Lord sitting on a throne, high and lifted up, and the train of His robe filled the temple. Above it stood seraphim; each one had six wings; with two he covered his face, with two he covered his feet, and with two he flew. And one cried to another and said, "Holy, holy, holy is the Lord of hosts; The whole earth is full of His glory!" And the posts of the door were shaken by the voice of him who cried out, and the house was filled with smoke.

Redeemed Dancing

As I remember the Redeemed dancing, some of the moves they made in praise reminded me of ballet, while other movements may have been part of a gymnastic routine. Some movements looked like jumping, running, hopping, and rolling. Many brought back to my remembrance different dances that I have seen from other countries other than the United States. Some dance moves that I saw, I knew I would never have words to describe on earth. They were performed with great love and beauty. That I did know. The Father's face had a big smile as He looked upon those dancing before Him. Yes, I remember that smile.

There were more and more moves of creation to God in dancing. There was dancing from the inner essence of Heaven to the highest parts of God's Glory. As I looked at the beauty of the dancing from all of God's creation, I remembered how I danced with them. The intensity seemed to increase within me, as if dancing itself was alive in every performance of praise I did. As I remembered all of us before the Throne of God, every creation was doing some form of dance in worship before God Almighty with great love.

I remembered the intense joy that was coming out of me in dance. Every movement I made was praise to my Father. I remember waving my hands in a dance and feeling like a small child moving with the wind on a windy day. As the wind would increase in speed, I felt like I could fly. But since I am back on this earth, this longing for such joy in praise seems impossible for me to achieve. When I was in Heaven, I had no limitations in honoring my Father in dancing.

Back in that hospital room, I thought about the grasses and flowers in their dancing to God. Actually, I thought about everything that happened in that dance before the Throne of God. This dancing to praise God was not part of my belief of how we would celebrate Him in Heaven before I died. I just believed we would all sing to Him, not dance.

I knew dancing was a way to express how much you loved God, but to me, it was not a major way to show Him love. Yet, King David danced before God in celebrating the coming into Jerusalem of the Ark of the Covenant.

2 SAMUEL 6:14-17 (NKJV)

Then David danced before the Lord with all his might; and David was wearing a linen ephod. So David and all the house of Israel brought up the ark of the Lord with shouting and with the sound of the trumpet. Now as the ark of the Lord came into the City of David, Michal, Saul's daughter, looked through a window and saw King David leaping and whirling before the Lord; and she despised him in her heart. So they brought the ark of the Lord, and set it in its place in the midst of the tabernacle that David had erected for it. Then David offered burnt offerings and peace offerings before the Lord.

Struggling Back on Earth

I remember struggling back on earth with my thinking while trying to accept what I had experienced in Heaven. Within me, I knew I had been a part of what was genuine praise because of the unity I felt and witnessed. I saw and experienced what it was like to be a part of the pure passion for my Father. Because of this, I could see the real meaning of giving God our worship in love.

To see the honor coming out of God's creations and knowing that it does not end was amazing. The dance, the praise, the thundering booms, and the songs coming from each creation of God were eternal. There was no end to the praise that came from each being in Heaven.

So I knew dancing could be a celebration of God, but experiencing it in Heaven raised it to a different level for me. It opened my eyes to see how many ways creation, even on earth, could show Him love.

I remember when I arrived home after leaving the hospital. I had many adjustments to make if I were to live back on this planet. One of my predicaments was I disliked sleeping lying down. I was very uncomfortable in doing it. It took me some time to adapt back to lying down to sleep. The first few months, I would try to lie down, but I would only last for an hour or two. What helped me through this situation was looking forward to the day awakening.

Being in Heaven and experiencing all of God's creation coming before Him in a song or a dance had caused me to not want to sleep. This apprehension about sleeping was, to me, my fight with darkness. Life was so intensified in pure praise in Heaven that I only wanted to live in the Light with no need to sleep.

So I looked forward to the dawning of each new day. Many

mornings I would wait for the sun to rise over the horizon, The Day Awaken, as I named it. I would get out of bed, while it was still dark, and sit on our couch in the family room with the blinds open so that I could see the sun come up over the horizon.

The first light of the day to me was a call to praise, and everything on earth knew it. I would hear the birds start their chirping and tweeting, followed by other sounds that would fill the air. The circle of the sun had not yet become visible, but the rays of light I could see, and the dark sky gave way to yellows, oranges, reds, and white. The early morning blue appeared with a dash of violet.

All of this taking place in the morning would comfort me at that time, because it reminded me of how all of God's Creation came together in one accord to rejoice because of Him. I wanted to be a part of that early morning praise.

By being in Heaven and performing a dance of joy, I came to know all of life has a reason to thank God for their very existence.

PSALM 150:1-6 (NKJV)

Praise the Lord! Praise God in His sanctuary; Praise Him in His mighty firmament! Praise Him for His mighty acts; Praise Him according to His excellent greatness! Praise Him with the sound of the trumpet; Praise Him with the lute and harp! Praise Him with the timbrel and dance; Praise Him with stringed instruments and flutes! Praise Him with loud cymbals; Praise Him with clashing cymbals! Let everything that has breath praise the Lord. Praise the Lord!

CHAPTER 12

Worship Comes from the Essence of Life

Liquid Fire

As the music was still sounding, creations in Heaven were still singing songs of love. Others were dancing and rejoicing to the sounds of praise. As I stared at the Throne of God suspended in the heavens, I saw a form of liquid-LIKE material underneath it.

This watery substance under the Throne was starting to rise and move in a dance-LIKE movement. This material looked like a lake of liquid fire but was something more than liquid. It seemed to be more like fire at times and at other times, more like a watery substance. Even though it resembled a liquid form, it was not molten lava. In both forms, it started to rise into the atmosphere, looking like a massive wave. It rose past the mountains, the colors, and even the sky of Heaven itself. How high it reached in praise is out of my ability to explain. As it rose, parts of it seemed to detach and fall back to the base of the fire-LIKE lake under the Throne. As this part of it fell, I heard a sound of praise like a loud whistle. I know this sound was the lake of fire making music in praise to its Creator. As long as praise was going on, this fire-LIKE substance under the Throne kept making this movement in adoration to God. It never was taller than God Almighty. It never even came close to being bigger than Him. I knew this fiery lake under the Throne was God's pure glory. I knew it was the perfect glory of Jesus. I knew it was the real glory of the Spirit of Holiness. This liquid-LIKE form of fire was God's glory giving Him praise. It was His Consuming Fire.

Seas

The fire-LIKE lake under the Throne was different than any of the rivers in Heaven. It was not the same as the seas that looked like crystal glass whose colors were closer to a majestic white. They all had their way of dancing and moving in praise to God Almighty. The watery substance of the blazing liquid material under the Throne was different than that of the rivers and the seas.

All of them seemed to dance with a different song sung to God. As each creation sang its song of love to God Almighty, there was a dance going on between the glass-LIKE seas before the Throne and the different songs of praise to Him. The seas seem to sway back and forth like a gentle breeze moves on the surface of a lake. It glistened as it moved with many colors coming from Father God. Each color would seem to melt within the seas. They did not become one, but they appeared to be dancing together. I saw reds, blues, oranges, yellows, greens, purples, violets, and some other colors. Some I could recognize, and others I was not familiar with. The seas kept their gentle swaying even when dancing with the colors. They never took on a form that resembled a storm crossing an ocean. This was their way of giving their God, their Creator, praise. Many of us, the Redeemed, would move to the same motion in worshipping our Father. I knew the sea's dance was giving love and affection with each move.

Rivers

The third watery form that was in Heaven was the rivers of Heaven. Some look like rivers you see on earth while others resembled rivers of fire. The rivers had a dance that was different than the seas of Heaven or the fiery lake under the Throne. The rivers would meet the love songs in the skies of Heaven before they reached God and danced with sounds of praise as they advanced upward to the Father of creation. The one thing that was unique about the rivers dancing before the Throne is that they danced with the songs of love. I did not see any other creation of God dance like this in any form or way. They would form themselves into a flute-LIKE instrument. As the songs ascended to God Almighty, the rivers shaped themselves into flute-LIKE shapes and wrapped around the individual sounds of praise coming to God. By making themselves into flutes, they enhanced the sounds of thanks coming from the children of God. I could hear the sounds going through the watery-LIKE flutes and see the wonderfully magnified sounds that came out. They, the rivers of Heaven, would add their love to the love from the singer. So together with the singers, the rivers' love dance, and also the colors of glory from the Throne, God received individual forms of love from the different creations in serving each other. The water did not dance with every sound, but when it did, oh how beautiful it did sound in praise to God Almighty!

The fiery rivers also had a way of dancing with the songs of praise. They made themselves into a ring of fire in the atmosphere above the seas. As each of these circles of fire made a ring, a vibration would produce another sound of love toward the Father. There was a ring coming from the glowing as if someone were ringing a bell. Each ring or sound coming from the fire rings would look like sound waves moving upward to God. One after another of these fiery rings of sound advanced to the Throne. When they reached my Father, they deposited the songs of love from the creation to Him. He seemed to receive the sounds of love in His hands. I saw God extended His hands in love to take the love given to Him.

In the Hospital

I remembered back in my room in the hospital how it seemed like the rivers that resembled flutes were playing the songs of praise. As I stated earlier, it reminded me of somebody playing the piano, but it was not a piano that the rivers formed. It was a flute or flutes. The songs that were sung by the Redeemed seemed to meet with the watery flutes. The rivers did not play with all of those who sang a song to God. As I was thinking about all of what took place with the rivers before the Throne, it looked to me like the rivers concentrated on the sounds of love from the Redeemed.

I recalled the song that I had sung. The rivers danced with my music and songs that I had produced in praise to my Father. How it seemed to me that I could feel the water wrapping itself around my sound of praise. It was like I was being wrapped with this incredible feeling of love for my Father. Oh, how I love Him! I remember the Holy Spirit on the inside of me helping me to show that love to Him in song, dance, and music. This water that wrapped itself around my praise to God seemed to be in accord with me in loving my Father. It appeared to be in much harmony with me in showing love through dance and sound. Because of this combining of love from the river and me, I wanted to increase my production of pure love for God Almighty. The experience of offering up a song of praise to Him made me feel like I was the song, wrapped up by the watery flutes.

I also, remember seeing how the musical sounds, thoughts, songs and watery flutes were all joined by the colors coming off of God Almighty. As the colors would descend from Him, they would dance their way down to the musical sounds of praise rising. Since the flutes of water had already surrounded the love songs, I saw the colors joined with them all to dance in praise to my Father, God Almighty.

As I thought about the rivers, I remembered seeing the sea that is in Revelation 4:6 in the Bible, the sea that is before the Throne of God. John, the writer of Revelation wrote that it "looked something like a sea of glass, like crystal." I was thinking how over the years I had heard people say that they had a vision of Heaven. They say they saw the crystal sea. I thought to myself, "It was not crystal, it looked LIKE crystal, but it was not." All these years, I had an image of glass-LIKE sea before the Throne that was not there. There is a sea that shines like glass or crystal. It has so many beautiful colors reflecting off of it that make it look like a mirror, but it is just an incredible, beautiful, lovely sea before the Throne of my Father.

As I thought about all this love from the Consuming Fire Lake, the seas, and many rivers, I remembered all of the praise that was rising to the Creator at the same moment. None of it was competing against another form of tribute, as I said before.

Praise of each kind was so different every moment. No one creation appeared to do the same thing in giving praise to God Almighty. Each dance, song, musical sound, and thought was new every moment. I remember thinking how outstanding, wonderful, and magnificent it all was. There were no repeated words or sounds of praise given to God Almighty. If the praise was a jump, it was presented in a bound again in a different manner. If a gymnastic move was made in the dance, the gymnastics praise was done differently the next moment. If it looked as if it were a ballet move, it was done in a different fashion the next moment they danced. Every kind of praise given to God from His creation gave its thankfulness in an intensity of worship that told the Creator they loved and appreciated Him from an increasing love. The praise to God Almighty was expressed through love dances, love songs, love musical sounds, and love thoughts.

REVELATION 4:6 (NKJV)
(SEA)

Before the throne there was a sea of glass, like crystal. And in the midst of the throne, and around the throne, were four living creatures full of eyes in front and in back.

REVELATION 15:2 (NKJV)
(SEA OF FIRE)

And I saw something like a sea of glass mingled with fire, and those who have the victory over the beast, over his image and over his mark and over the number of his name, standing on the sea of glass, having harps of God.

REVELATION 22:1 (NKJV)
(RIVER)

And he showed me a pure river of water of life, clear as crystal, proceeding from the throne of God and of the Lamb.

DANIEL 7:10 (NKJV)
(RIVER OF FIRE/FIERY)

A fiery stream issued And came forth from before Him. A thousand thousands ministered to Him; Ten thousand times ten thousand stood before Him. The court was seated, And the books were opened.

PSALMS 98:4-9 (NKJV)

Shout joyfully to the Lord, all the earth; Break forth in song, rejoice and sing praises. Sing to the Lord with the harp, With the harp and the sound of a psalm, With trumpets and the sound of a horn; Shout joyfully before the Lord, the King. Let the sea roar, and all its fullness, The world and those who dwell in it; Let the rivers clap their hands; Let the hills be joyful together before the Lord, for He is coming to judge the earth. With righteousness He shall judge the world, And the peoples with equity.

CHAPTER 13

Worship Is from the Beginning

Beings of Praise

In addition to the liquid fire, the seas, and the rivers around the Throne of God there were these other beings with six wings. They existed to be in the place where I saw them, around Him. These wonderful creations of God stood out with such beauty to me. It was not that they were more beautiful than any other creation, because God knows how to make everything beautiful. Anything He creates is beautiful, but I just remember that I could only see how beautiful they were. I could experience the beauty of these creations of God. I experienced them in the dance they did. I felt them in the songs they sang. I encountered them in the beautiful music they made. I knew them in the peaceful love sound they gave. I experienced the very thought of praise they handed to my Father.

There was an aroma that went along with their praise and worship that I cannot forget. All that is in Heaven gave Him a peaceful smell of adoration. Even I did, when I worshipped my Father in a song of love. I just remember that praise and the smell of love went together in Heaven. I was aware of the praise, aroma, and beauty of every creation that I encountered. Because of their elegance and peaceful smell, I just wanted to join in with them as they praised Him.

Beings of Beauty

These six-winged beings, with many hands under each wing, had eyes that seemed to be all over their bodies. Some of these beings were very tall and big. Others were very short and small. Their legs appeared to be longer than their bodies.

Their chests were covered with so many, and I mean so many, beautiful jewel-LIKE stones. These jewel-LIKE stones seemed to change color and shape as they gave their praise to God Almighty. At some moments, the jewels looked to melt together to become one large stone.

The brilliance of the wings in color is indescribable from an earthly point of view. Some of the feather-LIKE wings seemed to consist of all kinds and shades of colors. Red seemed to be the dominant color of these creations of God. Yet green seemed at moments to be the dominant color. The shades of color upon each wing and feather were so bright and brilliant. The colors appeared to give off their praise with every move these beings made. As they moved back and forth or up and down, they released praise toward the Throne in which God Almighty sat. With each up and down motion made with the wings, I saw praise come from the very atmosphere to Him. It was as if the wings and atmosphere were creating sounds of praise for God Almighty. What a beautiful sound they made together. I have no way to express the sounds they formed. It was a pure expression of love that they had for their Creator.

The eyes that each of these beautiful creations had all over them were of different sizes. Some of the eyes were big, and some were smaller in size. The eyes seemed to blink in sequence with the motion of the wings and the atmosphere in giving praise to God. With each blink of praise, there appeared to come out of each eye an element of love for their God. The praise seemed to look and sound like waves of water moving in the atmosphere. At times they appeared to blink together, and at other occasions, they all blinked at different moments. I saw that each eye created a new praise with each blink.

Creation of New Praise

These beautiful creations of God worshipped Him with new praises of love and adoration. They did not create these moments of worship, but the Creator of Love constructed these new praises for them in love. God was making it easier for them to give Him praise. He had made each moment easier for each being to give Him praise. These newly created tributes of praise that came from the beings moved me. What an incredible substance of love!

Perfect Praise Forever

I looked at those beautiful creations of God as they flapped their wings and gave a new song to their Creator in love. I saw multitudes upon multitudes of them. How many there were, I cannot find a number that is big enough to speak or would capture how many. I could not even think of how many were around God Almighty, giving Him honor and praise every new moment. And yet, I knew that they were created to give that perfect pitch of sound in praise with their mouths, wings, and blinking eyes. This was their purpose to praise in perfect sound to God Almighty forever.

Even after the great multitude of creations and I returned to our places in Heaven to fulfill our purpose of worship, these beings were created to be before the Throne. These created creatures of God are still at the Throne of God praising Him. They would stay dancing around the Throne of God in worship. They would sing a new song of praise to Him every moment. They were created to keep praising God high up in the atmosphere and in the glory of His creation, giving Him their perfect praise forever.

In the Hospital

When I was in my hospital room thinking about that moment when I was there in that worship of praise looking at those brilliant and beautiful creations of God, I remembered how they looked with their beautiful wings. All I could think of was how those wings moved back and forward, up and down, and how each feather seemed alive. This movement showed me a sense of how wonderfully I was made to give my Father praise.

Every detail of those beings of God was beautiful. They did not look like anything I have ever encountered on earth. In fact, I knew others on earth would say they were ugly and even grotesque. But all I saw was pure love in a creation of God. Since there is no fear in Heaven, there was no other way I could see them. I thought to myself, how much detail it took to create those beautiful beings of praise. How God Almighty gave His very best in making them. Others might find fault with how those creations looked, yet I know God did not create any mistakes in how He made them. They were perfectly made to worship and praise Him.

I then thought about us, human beings. We are made in His image. We that call Him Father were created to be with Him forever. He made the mouth that I speak with and the very sound of my voice to give a song of love to Him. My lips were made to deliver words of praise to my Heavenly

Father. His ears were made to hear me. Every part of me was put together to give Him perfect praise now. Again, it hit me! Every part of me was to give Him praise now!

PSALM 99:1-3 (NKJV)

The Lord reigns; Let the peoples tremble! He dwells between the cherubim (winged angels); Let the earth be moved! The Lord is great in Zion, And He is high above all the peoples. Let them praise Your great and awesome name—He is holy.

CHAPTER 14

Worship Brings Glory

Glory from Above

Above my Father was a cloud, a bright cloud that seemed to look like it was coming out of God Himself, and yet, I knew that it was Him. It was another form of His glory, different than the glory below the Throne. The glory above Him looked like blazing red and white clouds as if the sun were setting and reflecting a bright light off of them, but that was not the case. The colors were coming from the glory clouds themselves. They also resembled big puffy storm clouds that extended in the skies of Heaven. How high they went, I cannot tell you. I knew that if I looked forever, I would not have been able to see the end of them.

Just picture this… Below Him was a fiery lake of His glory and above Him there were fiery clouds of His glory. Praise be to the Lord!

Life Giving Glory

To watch this honor of praise for God was like seeing life given out. It seemed like this glory above brought life to all of us in Heaven. I do not know how to explain it, but it appears the essence of life was in the glory of God; and when it celebrated the Creator, life took on a new and greater meaning for me.

I saw the clouds take on various shapes to praise God. At times, the clouds of glory looked like tornadoes spinning up around Him. As I saw them spring up, I wanted to be a part of the windstorm of His glory and joy. I wanted to dance within those twisters of praise.

I kept my eyes on my Father and saw the greatness moving around Him, and then it started to come down to where I was. As this glory reached me, it surrounded me. I was in the eye of His glory and sheer praise. What joy I experienced, what love I felt, what splendor became a part of me! Life took on magnificent holiness to me.

Surrounded by His Glory

This glory came to each of us. Each creation of God was surrounded with a brilliance of blazing light. What honor this form of a cloud was bringing each and every one of us. We were in the joy, and we were the joy.

In the Hospital

In my hospital room, I remembered the smell that God's living glory had. It was like a fresh breeze smell coming off the ocean. At the same time, it was like smells coming from a mountain pasture full of wildflowers and grasses with a slight smell of a water spring. I just remember how relaxed I was, thinking, just thinking of that moment in Heaven.

I recalled when I was in Heaven and the glory cloud was all around me. I knew that this cloud was His glory, the glory that we all strive to be a part of, a beauty that only God can create. Within this glory cloud, there seemed to be an echoing sound of brightness. There was glory on glory within glory. This light gave praise to God the Father, and as it did, it was an everlasting praise. I knew this as I heard the sound of God's glory giving God praise for being God Almighty. New beauty came into being. I understood this was reoccurring at the same moment other glory existed. There was no end to this self-grandeur of praise for my Father. In the midst of this great glory cloud, I saw a river of heavenly water moving to a point where it stood up and rose into the atmosphere and formed what looked like a waterfall. The difference was the water was flowing from the heavenly holy ground upward. I saw it rising high in the sky in such a beautiful shape. In the motion of ascending, it was sending praise out to all of Heaven. In its praising God, His glory was moving away from Him. There seemed to be more praise clouds of glory moving out and forming into some dance. This dance of beauty looked like rolls of circles around rolls of circles. These glory clouds rose up and then fell to the ground. They would perform this move quickly and connect with the fiery lake of His glory under the Throne.

Glory for God Only

The sounds the glory clouds were creating in praising God were another musical creation that was new every moment. I knew there was no other reason for this radiance even to exist but to give Him praise forever. How do I describe these sounds of glory that do not come from this planet? They were more wonderful and beautiful than any English words that I can produce or could come out of my mouth.

With the lake of fire below the Throne of God and the clouds above, I knew at that moment that glory was created only for God. Glory had no other reason to be but for God Almighty.

The Throne of Glory

Even His Throne is Glory. I heard it singing a beautiful song of praise to God Almighty. It looks like a cloud or better yet, a well-built mist moving over the liquid lake of fire. My Father was looking like He was sitting on a cloud Throne. Now this Throne was singing a song of praise to the One who sat on it. Again what a beautiful song it was. I saw the glory of God moving in and out, all around and throughout God's Throne. God's glory carried a beat with it. Everything that was near the Throne moved in the beat praising God. I knew as I lived in Heaven that the Throne was God Himself, and yet it had its own life, a life that could give praise in song.

Months Later

As I was reading in Revelation I came across where it says the Throne was talking. I have thought to myself since then that God's Throne is much more than a chair to sit on. It is also a lot more than what we can imagine.

REVELATION 19:4-5 (NKJV)

And the twenty-four elders and the four living creatures fell down and worshipped God who sat on the throne, saying, "Amen! Alleluia!" Then a voice came from the throne, saying, "Praise our God, all you His servants and those who fear Him, both small and great!"

PSALMS 19:1 (NKJV)

The heavens declare the glory of God; And the firmament shows His handiwork.

Firmament: the vault of heaven; sky.

PSALMS 93:1-5 (NKJV)

The Lord reigns, He is clothed with majesty; The Lord is clothed, He has girded Himself with strength. Surely the world is established, so that it cannot be moved. Your throne is established from of old; You are from everlasting. The floods have lifted up, O Lord, The floods have lifted up their voice; The floods lift up their waves. The Lord on high is mightier Than the noise of many waters, Than the mighty waves of the sea. Your testimonies are very sure; Holiness adorns Your house, O Lord, forever.

CHAPTER 15

Worship Leads
to a Life Song

The Creation of Love

Then He, my Father, God the Creator of everything, looked at me with such love and opened His mouth. When He opened His mouth, He started to sing. My Father was singing to me. He was singing a new love song to me. He was singing a life song to me. I saw that song of love coming from His holy mouth, and yet I heard it coming from deep within Him. It was a beautiful song full of life. It seemed to roll from His lips like an enormous waterfall coming off a tall mountain or like an avalanche of white snow coming down the side of a high cliff.

Anticipation

I can remember the anticipation I had of what was coming my way. It was the gift of love made just for me. It was a love song with everything I needed to live by and everything I needed to exist in.

As my Father produced this song of love for me, I seemed to

119

grow in life. It was like every fiber, every core, and every living thread woven together that made me was being impacted by God in the making of my song. It was pure affection for this son of His. Joy, truth, goodness, kindness, gentleness, strength, fulfillment, happiness, and just being accepted for who I was, one of His offspring, were all included in that love. That fun love song made personally for me seemed to grow in life and love as it approached me. Even before it reached me, my Father was still working on this love song. It was not that it wasn't that perfect when it left Him. It was that anything my Father created has life producing ability to generate more zest and passion. I knew this process was still God Almighty, orchestrating this life-giving affection, targeted toward me!

As this song of love and life was coming toward me, everything in me jumped to a different level of being prepared to receive this sound of love, my sound. It appeared that all of a sudden, I was being transformed to respond in a greater way to Him like never before.

All of Me Could Hear the Sound of Love

My eyes seemed to not only see the song coming from my Father, but they could also listen to the sound. I was able to hear with my eyes. This song that I could see headed towards me.

As I heard the sound, it was filled with so much life. It was also light blue in color. It looked to be riding on a color of red with some orange mixed in with it. All I could hear and see with my eyes was how much He loved me, even before the love song created just for me reached me. I also heard the song with my spiritual ears in a pureness not found on earth. This sound was so different than what I listened to with my eyes. Even though I could still hear it with my eyes, my ears heard a soft instrumental sound of trumpets. The music I listened to with my eyes was more like a piano. Each part of me heard the song differently than another segment of me. But one thing the warm sound carried with it was pure life, love, joy, and serenity.

Love Grown of Its Self

As this song of life and love came closer, it looked to grow in life, love, joy, and serenity. At the same time, it was as if I were growing bigger in all the life-giving attributes of my Father. I knew I was His child, and He was and is my Father. But all at once, I became His son of love. I knew I was before, but now I was His son created to receive His song of love, my song of life. Again, this was before the life song of love reached me. I wanted to hold my created love song, my created life song. It was like this was the first time I was to receive my Father's love. I had received His love every moment I had life on Earth and in Heaven, but this was different.

The Drawing of God's Love Song

As this song of life moved toward me, I moved toward it. I was being drawn to the song, and I was pulling the song to me. I had not moved from where I was, bowing before the Throne, but it seemed as if I were moving toward the love song of life. As His love song came closer and closer, everything about me lit up with greater serenity, greater joy, greater love, and greater life. My happiness seemed to grow, also, as the love and life song got closer. I even appeared to have a greater love for my Father, the Lord Jesus Christ, and the life-giving Holy Spirit residing on the inside of me. As my life song of love got closer to me, it was different from any song I had heard or seen before.

Enhanced Senses

I now realized I was not only hearing the song with my spiritual body, but I heard it with the rest of my senses (taste, smell, touch, sight, feelings). I also could see it with all my senses. My senses of taste, smell, touch, sight, and feelings were gathering every bit of information they could in Heaven. They all seemed so adaptive to each other's abilities. I could not only hear with my eyes, but I could taste, smell, and touch with my eyes. Every one of my five senses could do what the rest of the senses were made to do on earth. As my song of life came closer, all of my enhanced senses picked up an increasing, roaring sound; but I could still hear and see with all my abilities. It was a beautiful harmonic sensitive song of love that was created just for my whole being. I don't know if others heard it as I heard my song, but it didn't matter at all to me. I knew my sounds that came out of my Father's mouth had been created for me and only me. Everything about me could hear the song of love created for me with love.

By the time it reached me, my song was huge in size. As it reached me, everything about the song of love filled every portion of my being. I was already alive, and yet it seemed like now I had even more life.

God Creates New Songs Every Moment

I knew that every creation in Heaven and on Earth had its own song of life and love made for it. I knew as the song started to enter in that anytime we sing to God Almighty, He creates a song of love and life for those who are singing to Him. Each song created by Him was new, freshly created for the one who sang to Him.

I came to this knowledge as my song of love started to

penetrate into me. I did not need to see or even hear the love songs of life to know this. I knew because of the way my Father took so much care in creating my song of life.

As my song of life started to enter into my being, it was not just coming in through my ears, but through everything that could hear my song. I was like a sponge soaking up every bit of my sound of love. I knew it was penetrating my senses in every way. It was like one big key that became many small keys unlocking every single part of me. As I became open or undone, I also became whole in a moment. It was life within the life of my song that came from my Father. The song electrified everything about me with a new sense of love, joy, excitement, and comfort. It seemed as if the song became a part of me, and I became a part of the song in an instant. As the song moved inside my being, it was like air in my lungs on earth and blood flooding through my veins with some form of warmth. All I knew was that this was my song of praise and love that was sung to me, given to me, and made for me. I wanted all of it and could not have existed without it.

I Am Made for God's Song

Even before my ears lived, they wanted to hear this song. They longed for this music. This pure song of love penetrated my eyes as it reached me. My eyes and ears were created for that moment when that song entered into them, I knew. The scent of the song of life was within the very essence of a perfect fragrance for me. As this song of love and life touched me I knew I was made to fit within the song and the song was made to fit inside me. The taste of my created love song of life filled my need for energy to sustain me.

The Holy Spirit Contacting
with the Song of Love

When my love song of life reached my most inner being, it came in contact with the Holy Spirit in me. Once it came in touch with the God on the inside of me, there was an explosion of love on the inside of me. I knew at that moment that my Father loved me and that love would always be! I knew that He has always loved me, and even when I was just a thought, before I was formed inside my mother, He loved me.

I also came to accept that my Father creates a new love for me every moment. He does not love me with the same love every second, but with newly created love that He creates every instant. Every part of my being was built for this glorious and continuous love song.

My Turn to Sing

As the song of love reached God's Spirit within me, I knew it was my turn to send a song of love from me with the help of the Spirit of Holiness back to my Father. I had the full knowledge of how to build a perfect song of love back to Him. I understood that this is what every created being in Heaven did when their love song of life reached them and became a part of them. Every moment the Father sings to us, we sing back to Him an individual love song. He did this many times. He sings countless love songs, at the same time to so many. Countless and varied are the songs of love coming out of God Almighty for each and every creation in Heaven. If I said there were billions upon billions upon billions of love songs of life coming from the Creator at the same time to each creation, I still would be way short in the numbers of songs created by my Father.

The Creator of Love Songs

My Father, my God, can and did sing a created love song of life to each creation as if they were the only one singing to Him. Now all creations in Heaven would and did sing back a personal love song to Him. He received a created deep love song from all of us, with the help of the Holy Spirit.

He sang; we sang. My Father sang; I sang. The great Creator of love songs, sang to all of us in Heaven, and we would sing our created love songs back to Him.

In the Hospital

When I was in my room in the hospital, I thought about that moment when my Father sang back to me. The whole scene reminded me of a Bible book named the Song of Solomon, or Song of Songs. In this book, you have two people expressing their love for each other through songs and poems. I can remember reading the book knowing it was about the Beloved to the Lover, each showing their love for one another. The Beloved would sing a song of love to the Lover, and the Lover in return would sing a love song back to the Beloved. This went on throughout the book. It is a beautiful exchange of emotional love songs between two people who loved each other.

In the Jewish tradition, it is a metaphor of the bond between God and Israel. Christian tradition reads the poem as an image of Christ and His bride, the church.

My Love Song for my Father and His Love Song for Me

That is how it seemed to me. I would sing to my Father, and He would sing a love song back to me. There was a beat with each exchange of songs between my Father and me. It was something like the beat that pulls everything in Heaven together, and yet it was its own beat. This exchange of love went back and forth for what seemed like a long time, but as I reflect on it, it seemed like it was only a moment of my life there. I knew that every creation of life was created to love God Almighty with their whole heart, soul, strength, and mind. I knew that I had that ability, and there I got to sing it to Him!

Coming Home from Canada

About a month after coming home from the hospital. My wife and I went to Canada for a weekend trip. We needed some time to be alone after going through the whole ordeal of my dying for 1 hour and 45 minutes. We only stayed a day in Canada and then started back to Federal Way, Washington, where we lived then.

On the way back, we stopped at a Christian bookstore in between Custer and Ferndale Washington. We bought the latest Israel Houghton and New Bread CD at that time. As we listened to it, I heard Israel make the statement that the Lord sings over us, and he said it was found in the Zephaniah in the Bible. When I heard this, I got so excited. I did not know up to that moment that the Bible even said that God sings over us. Again, here was another proof of what I had experienced in the Word of God. That is why I say my story does not prove the Bible, but that the Bible proves my story.

ZEPHANIAH 3:17 (NKJV)

The Lord your God in your midst, The Mighty One, will save; He will rejoice over you with gladness, He will quiet you with His love, He will rejoice over you with singing."

PSALM 59:16-17 (NKJV)

But I will sing of Your power; Yes, I will sing aloud of Your mercy in the morning; For You have been my defense And refuge in the day of my trouble. To You, O my Strength, I will sing praises; For God is my defense, My God of mercy.

CHAPTER 16

Worship Awakens the Day

The Glory of Praise Within

As the moments went on in praising, the singing seemed to become greater and lovelier for my Father, the Creator. I also wanted to give Him more love in song and praise. I wanted to give this great love I had for Him with such compassion. It was like every moment, this love I had for God bonded us even closer. How that could be? I cannot explain, but that is the impression I had. I praised God, my Father, from an endless source of passion produced inside of me with the help of His Spirit of Holiness.

In the Hospital

In the hospital room, I thought of that intensifying love within me. I had to question myself. How could I love God that much every moment? My love for Him appeared to increase in ways that surpassed anything I had experienced for Him previously. The other question I had for myself was, "How could I love God Almighty, my Father, that purely?" That experience of love and life was new to me. The closest I can come to explaining what it felt like to me is to share how I experienced a sunrise on a clear blue day.

Sunrise

I have always loved the mornings of the day. Without exception, it seemed to bring me closer to life. This powerful love I had for God reminded me of seeing the sun rising on a cloudless morning and how I would feel the excitement of the day starting with life. The more light that showed as the sun came over the horizon, the more I seemed to engage with the life and love of the day. I recall how those first rays of warm light that crossed my face, always appeared to cause me to smile with such zeal. I even felt the smile forming on my face. I seemed to know in those moments that I was loved, and I needed to love. I thought of those times, while in the hospital room, of the sun topping the horizon and how I would form a smile on my face. It brought me back to how much joy and love I experienced during those times on earth.

As each moment showed more of the sun coming over the horizon, the anticipation of joy grew within me. As I recall, that is how that love of worship seemed to be reacting to the love of praise rising on the inside of me. It was like a sunrise coming up within me. As the love enlarged within me, the closer it came to coming out of me. My joy became greater for God.

The Day Awakens

Because of the great love I had encountered in Heaven, when I was back at home in Federal Way, Washington, I wanted to get up every morning to see what I called, The Day Awakens. I wrote a little about this earlier. I would make sure I would be up early in the morning, sitting in my family room on the couch, looking through the windows into our dark backyard, before it was light. I wanted to see and hear the day awaken.

I remember how the birds would start their chirping and tweeting as the darkness made way for the light. I remember how I experienced the joy of being a part of giving praise to my Father Almighty as THE DAY AWAKENS. The birds seemed to get louder with each new light. I would see that beautiful yellow, orange, and red light take over the dark sky before it became blue. It sounded to me like all of life was praising their Creator. At that moment, every bird wanted the world to know in praise that God made the light, God made the air, and God made them. It was as if I could hear and sense other creatures and things producing various sounds of praise as the dawn gave way to life. Besides the birds chirping or singing, some of those sounds would be the first breezes blowing through the trees. It even sounded like the trees would thank God as they moved in the wind.

I had a flower garden in my backyard and could hear all kinds of activity taking place when the light of the day became brighter. I might see the flowers opening up or turning to the sunrise as the rays first appeared to them. I might hear or see the bees buzzing as they moved in and around in the morning from flower to flower to gather pollen. All of this activity and the sounds to me at that moment were praise to my Father, God.

Through the Years

As I spent more time back on earth, I experienced sunrises throughout the United States and other countries (Trinidad and Tobago, Peru, Singapore, Canada, New Zealand, Australia, Northern Ireland, and Wales). In all of these places, I was able to hear different birds sing. Always the birds' songs at the beginning of the day appeared to give thanksgiving to God! Also, it would bring to my recall the sounds of praise I heard.

Stream, Rivers, Oceans

I can remember being in places where a stream or river was, as I was watching the sun come up over the horizon and listening to the water. It always seemed to me that the sound of the water changed when the light got brighter in the morning. Even the oceans appeared to change their sound of waves coming to a shore when the brightness of the sun would touch the water. Again to me, these were all praising God!

Out in the Country

I have been out in the country and on farms during sunrises. I have heard the many sounds of farm animals like dogs, cats, horses, donkeys, cows, sheep, goats, llamas, chickens, roosters, ducks, turkeys, etc.… Every sound they made to me, as the sun came up over the horizon, was praise for God Almighty. The same was with wild animals in the country. It just always reminded me of all the unique ways of praising God that took place in Heaven.

I remember how every creation of God would sing and dance in praise and worship to God Almighty with such love and compassion. Everything would sing a new song to Him in praise. No song was a duplicate song of thanksgiving, as I stated before. Each single word of praise was a new song to God Almighty.

Those times of waking up early to be a part of honoring my Father God became a way for me of learning to live on earth, or how I like to say it, walk on the planet.

All of those sounds I heard in the morning, no matter where I was on earth, seemed to be praising God Almighty as The Day Awakened.

Native American Flutes

I now play Native American flutes as I wrote earlier, and I love to play them in the morning. To me, it is one of the best ways I can make a sound of joy with increasing love and great compassion. It allows me to join in with all of God's creation on earth in praising Him. I seem not only to be able to hear the flute sound but to feel the wind coming out of me in love to produce a sound that vibrates off of my eardrums in pure praise to God Almighty. What a great way to start a day. What a great way to join in "The Day Awakening" in praise!

PSALMS 59:16-17 (NKJV)

But I will sing of Your power; Yes, I will sing aloud of Your mercy in the morning; For You have been my defense And refuge in the day of my trouble. To You, O my Strength, I will sing praises; For God is my defense, My God of mercy.

PSALM 148:7-14 (NKJV)

Praise the Lord from the earth, You great sea creatures and all the depths; Fire and hail, snow and clouds; Stormy wind, fulfilling His word; Mountains and all hills; Fruitful trees and all cedars; Beasts and all cattle; Creeping things and flying fowl; Kings of the earth and all peoples; Princes and all judges of the earth; Both young men and maidens; Old men and children. Let them praise the name of the Lord, For His name alone is exalted; His glory is above the earth and heaven. And He has exalted the horn of His people, The praise of all His saints—Of the children of Israel, A people near to Him. Praise the Lord!

CHAPTER 17

Worship from the Heart Always Brings True Joy

Joy Upon Joy

In a moment, all of Heaven knew that we needed to move back to our places in Heaven from where we were worshipping God Almighty. That place of where we were called from to come to the Throne to sing praise to our Father, our Creator, and our God Almighty.

We, His creation, were all returning to our purpose in Heaven to do the things we were created to do forever. Our steps or movements to return seemed to be done with more joy than what we came with to the Throne. It was not that we did not have great joy when we came to the Throne. All of us were looking forward to singing, dancing, clapping, jumping, and producing any motion or sound that would give honor to our God.

We had such joy, but we left with more. It was like the joy we had was great, but the next moment of joy was greater. I knew that as I left the Throne, I was moving into something newer. It is hard to put into words, it was like all we could experience was a great joy every moment and even greater joy the next moment. Every second was newer and newer in

Heaven. We were moving from joy to joy, from happiness to happiness, from love to love, and from glory to glory.

The Fiery Creation before the Throne

Another thing that happened as I moved away from the Throne of God is that I saw the fiery pillows come out of Him. They seemed to be taller and wider in size. They seem to be more like liquid flames to me at that moment. Again, they moved as though they were people, but they were not. They were pillars of glowing glory of brightness. The magnitude of the light coming from them would outshine the intensity of all the lights on the earth and in the universe put together. As their flames flickered in the heavenly sky, it seemed as if the atmosphere also flickered back. These living fiery creations now took up their place before the Throne of God Almighty.

I Was Home in Heaven

I remember after experiencing this great gathering of all of God's creation in Heaven and showing creative love to Him, I knew I was home. I knew that I belonged with His creation. I was and am one of His original loved ones. I connected with everything there in Heaven, and everything in Heaven became more connected with me. I had joined in that great showing of love to my Father, our Creator. I had the privilege of expressing pure love in song to Him with others who had the same agenda in mind. I am and have been connected to each and every love song that went forth to the Mighty Creator. I had settled in and was staying. I had come to the full understanding of my purpose for eternity, and it was to worship God the Father forever with everything I was.

Family in Heaven

As I returned to my place in Heaven, I went back down on my hands and knees. In a moment Jesus was there, standing before me again. I looked at Him and saw His love for me. Once again, He loved me with everything He is. I could not take my eyes off of Him until He looked away from me. I looked in the direction that He looked, and I saw my family that was already there in Heaven.

They also were returning from this majestic worship of our Father and now stood on the other side of Jesus. They had come to greet me into Heaven. I will write more on that in another book, but for now I want to relate the pureness of the joy they all had. They were filled with the happiness and tranquility of experiencing Jesus in a way that only a song can express.

In the Hospital

I remember later in the hospital how I came out of that moment with hope, reverence, and adoration for God the Father. I see how every word in the Bible is praise to God our Creator. Every word has a song within itself. For every word is part of a story or a song telling how great our God is! I saw the actual meaning of singing words that praise our God, the great Creator. They are not just words put to a beat of the music. These words of praise coming out of my mouth to my Father were words of eternal life and love. Some people have asked me, "What was the one thing that happened in Heaven that changed you forever?" I can say that this moment of celebrating was a big event in my life that changed me forever. This one moment of exchanging love in song with my Father God brought me to the reality of the one reason I am back on earth. I am a new creation in

Christ Jesus, and I know what it means to be a new creation who can still open my mouth and sing a love song to my God, my Savior, my Lord, my Father.

Later I Came to Understand

Later, I came to understand, through this moment of praising my Father around the Throne, that the only reason I have a mouth is to sing or talk to God. When God created Adam, even before Eve was created, He gave him a mouth. What was his mouth made for? His mouth was made to sing or communicate to his Father. His voice was made to be understood by his God. His ears were made to hear from his Creator. We are the perfect beings to hold conversations with God Almighty, our Creator.

We Were Created First with All the Ability to Communicate with God

GENESIS 2:7 (NKJV)

And the Lord God formed man of the dust of the ground, and breathed into his nostrils the breath of life; and man became a living being.

GENESIS 2:21-23 (NKJV)

And the Lord God caused a deep sleep to fall on Adam, and he slept; and He took one of his ribs, and closed up the flesh in its place. Then the rib which the Lord God had taken from man He made into a woman, and He brought her to the man. And Adam said: "This is now bone of my bones And flesh of my flesh; She shall be called Woman, Because she was taken out of Man."

How to Become a Part
of the Praise of Heaven

If you want to be a part of this praise in Heaven, you must be born again. To do that you have to confess with your mouth that Jesus is Lord and believe in your heart that God raised Him from the dead, and you will be saved!

Say the Following to Be Saved

Dear Father God, I ask You to forgive me of anything I have done wrong to You or others. I invite You to come and be a part of my life. I thank You for hearing me, forgiving me, and coming into my life. I give You all of my life now. I ask and declare all of this in the name of Jesus.

Hear His Song

If you said this and meant it in your heart, you are now saved! You will and can praise your heavenly Father right now. SO, SING and hear Him sing to you.

ROMANS 10:8-13 (NKJV)

But what does it say? "The word is near you, in your mouth and in your heart" that is, the word of faith which we preach: that if you confess with your mouth the Lord Jesus and believe in your heart that God has raised Him from the dead, you will be saved. For with the heart one believes unto righteousness, and with the mouth confession is made unto salvation. For the Scripture says, "Whoever believes on Him will not be put to shame." For there is no distinction between Jew and Greek, for the same Lord over all is rich to all who call upon Him. For "whoever calls on the name of the Lord shall be saved."

PSALM 84:1-12 (NKJV)

How lovely is Your tabernacle, O Lord of hosts! My soul longs, yes, even faints For the courts of the Lord; My heart and my flesh cry out for the living God. Even the sparrow has found a home, And the swallow a nest for herself, Where she may lay her young— Even Your altars, O Lord of hosts, My King and my God. Blessed are those who dwell in Your house; They will still be praising You. Selah Blessed is the man whose strength is in You, Whose heart is set on pilgrimage. As they pass through the Valley of Baca, They make it a spring; The rain also covers it with pools. They go from strength to strength; Each one appears before God in Zion. O Lord God of hosts, hear my prayer; Give ear, O God of Jacob! Selah O God, behold our shield, And look upon the face of Your anointed. For a day in Your courts is better than a thousand. I would rather be a doorkeeper in the house of my God Than dwell in the tents of wickedness. For the Lord God is a sun and shield; The Lord will give grace and glory; No good thing will He withhold From those who walk uprightly. O Lord of hosts, Blessed is the man who trusts in You!

Hebrew and Greek Words That Mean Worship

Unity in Worship

Now when I was in Heaven, I experienced some forms of Deep Worship. I remember how all of the creation in Heaven came together in UNITY and praised God in many ways.

What we call Worship is not all there is to Worship. Yet many of us still only see when we come together to sing as Worship. Singing is a form of Worship, but if we want to give the most to God, we have to understand that actions should go along with singing for true Worship.

JOHN 4:23-24 (NKJV)

"But the hour is coming, and now is, when the true worshippers will worship the Father in spirit and truth; for the Father is seeking such to worship Him. God is Spirit, and those who worship Him must worship in spirit and truth."

Expressions of Worshiping

The following are some of the expressions of worshiping that I experienced, saw, and did in Heaven. You can find them defined in seven Hebrew words and three Greek words.

WORSHIP (HEBREW)

There are seven most common Hebrew words used for "worship." These words are translated in many different ways: worship, praise, shout, bless, thanks, sing, enthusiastic, etc. Each word has a different meaning in how it is applied.

Barak

To kneel or bow as an act of glorification, to give reverence to God as an act of loyalty, implies a continual awareness-giving place to God, to be attuned to Him and His presence.

Psalm 34:1 (NKJV) I will bless (Barak) the Lord at all times; His praise shall continually be in my mouth.

Psalm 100:4 (NKJV) Enter into His gates with thanksgiving, and into His courts with praise. Be thankful to Him, and bless (Barak) His name.

Psalm 95:6 (NKJV) Oh come, let us worship and bow down; Let us kneel (Barak) before the Lord our Maker.

Halal

To shine or give the light of sound, but usually of color, to be clear, to praise, to make a show or be enthusiastic about, to glory in or brag upon, to be enthusiastically foolish about your worship of God as in Hallelujah.

Psalm 22:23 (NKJV) You who fear the Lord, praise (Halal) Him! All you descendants of Jacob, glorify Him, and fear Him, all you offspring of Israel!

Psalm 44:8 (NKJV) In God we boast (Halal) all day long, and praise Your name forever. Selah

Psalm 63:5 (NKJV) My soul shall be satisfied as with marrow and fatness, and my mouth shall praise (Halal) You with joyful lips.

Shachah

To depress or prostrate in reverence or loyalty to God, bow down, bend, fall flat, and humbly pray, to show fervent and zealous love.

Psalm 29:2 (NKJV) Give unto the Lord the glory due to His name; Worship (Shachah) the Lord in the beauty of holiness.

Psalm 66:4 (NKJV) All the earth shall worship (Shachah) You and sing praises to You; They shall sing praises to Your name." Selah

Psalm 95:6 (NKJV) Oh come, let us worship (Shachah) and bow down; Let us kneel before the Lord our Maker.

Tehillah

To sing hallal, a new song, a hymn of spontaneous or unplanned praise, adoration and thanksgiving glorifying God in song.

Psalm 34:1 (NKJV) I will bless the Lord at all times; His praise (Thillah) shall continually be in my mouth.

Psalm 40:3 (NKJV) He has put a new song in my mouth—praise (Thillah) to our God; Many will see it and fear, and will trust in the Lord.

Psalm 149:1 (NKJV) Praise the Lord! Sing to the Lord a new song, and His praise (Thillah) in the assembly of saints.

Towdah

An extension of the hand, statement, adoration, a choir of worshipers, confession, sacrifice of praise, thanksgiving.

> *Psalm 50:14 (NKJV) Offer to God thanksgiving (Towdah), and pay your vows to the Most High.*

> *Psalm 69:30 (NKJV) I will praise the name of God with a song, and will magnify Him with thanksgiving (Towdah).*

> *Psalms 100:4 (NKJV) Enter into His gates with thanksgiving (Towdah), and into His courts with praise. Be thankful to Him, and bless His name.*

Yadah

To use or stretch hands out or to physically throw a stone or arrow at or away, especially to worship with in praise of thankful, thanksgiving, or intensively.

> *Psalm 7:17 (NKJV) I will praise (Yadah) the Lord according to His righteousness, And will sing praise to the name of the Lord Most High.*

> *Psalm 18:49 (NKJV) Therefore I will give thanks (Yadah) to You, O Lord, among the Gentiles, and sing praises to Your name.*

> *Psalm 33:2 (NKJV) Praise (Yadah) the Lord with the harp; Make melody to Him with an instrument of ten strings.*

Zamar

To touch the strings or parts of a musical instrument, i.e. play upon it, to make music accompanied by the voice, to celebrate in song and music, give praise, sing forth praises, psalms.

Psalm 66:2 (NKJV) Sing out (KJV:Sing forth) (Zamar) the honor of His name; Make His praise glorious.

Psalm 71:22 (NKJV) Also with the lute I will praise You—and Your faithfulness, O my God! To You I will sing (Zamar) with the harp, O Holy One of Israel.

Psalm 144:9 (NKJV) I will sing a new song to You, O God; On a harp of ten strings I will sing praises (Zamar) to You,

Only Two Have Anything to Do with Music

Out of the seven words, only two have anything to do with music: zamar—which means to play an instrument as an expression of worship to God, and tehillah—which suggests singing a spontaneous song of praise to God out of an overflowing of the heart.

WORSHIP (GREEK)

There are three Greek words used in the New Testament for "worship." In contrast to the Hebrew words for worship, the three Greek words for "worship" have less to do with the way we posture ourselves before God. These words focus more on reverence and service.

Proskyneo

The most common word in the New Testament for "worship" is proskyneo. This word occurs 60 times in the New Testament, 57 of which are in the four gospels, Acts, and Revelation. The other three instances are in 1 Corinthians 14, and Hebrews 1 and 11.

PROSKYNEO: 1) To kiss the hand, in token of reverence. 2) Among the Asians, especially the Persians, to fall upon the knees and touch the ground with the forehead as an expression of profound reverence. 3) In the New Testament by kneeling or prostration to honor one. Now whether to express respect or to make supplication—used of homage shown to men and beings of superior rank, i.e.: to the Jewish high priests, to God, to Christ, to heavenly beings, and also to demons.

Again it originally carried with it the idea of subjects falling to kiss the ground before a king or kiss their feet. The literal definition means "to kiss, like a dog licking his master's hand, to fawn or crouch to, homage (do reverence to, adore): worship."

Matthew 4:10 (NKJV) Then Jesus said to him, "Away with you, Satan! For it is written, 'You shall worship (Proskyneo) the Lord your God, and Him only you shall serve.'"

Matthew 8:2 (NKJV) And behold, a leper came and worshipped (Proskyneo) Him, saying, "Lord, if You are willing, You can make me clean."

Mark 5:6 (NKJV) When he saw Jesus from afar, he ran and worshipped (Proskyneo) Him.

Luke 24:50-53 (NKJV) And He led them out as far as Bethany, and He lifted up His hands and blessed them. Now it came to pass, while He blessed them, that He was parted from them and carried up into heaven. And they worshipped (Proskyneo) Him, and returned to Jerusalem with great joy, and were continually in the temple praising and blessing God. Amen.

John 4:23 (NKJV) But the hour is coming, and now is, when the true worshippers (Proskyneo) will worship (Proskyneo) the Father in spirit and truth; for the Father is seeking such to worship (Proskyneo) Him.

Revelation 5:14 (NKJV) Then the four living creatures said, "Amen!" And the twenty-four elders fell down and worshipped (Proskyneo) Him who lives forever and ever.

Latreuo

The second most common word for "worship" in the New Testament is Latreuo, which appears 21 times.

LATREUO: 1) to serve for hire. 2) to serve, minister to, either to the gods or men and used alike of slaves and freemen a) in the NT, to render religious service or homage, to worship; b) to perform sacred services, to offer gifts, to worship God in the observance of the rites instituted for his worship. Again it means, "to render religious service of reverence." It is commonly translated as the word "serve" when referring to serving God.

Luke 4:8 (NKJV) And Jesus answered and said to him, "Get behind Me, Satan! For it is written, 'You shall worship (Latreuo) the Lord your God, and Him only you shall serve (Latreuo).' "

Acts 26:7 (NKJV) To this promise our twelve tribes, earnestly serving (Latreuo) God night and day, hope to attain. For this hope's sake, King Agrippa, I am accused by the Jews.

Romans 1:9 (NKJV) For God is my witness, whom I serve (Latreuo) with my spirit in the gospel of His Son, that without ceasing I make mention of you always in my prayers,

2 Timothy 1:3 (NKJV) I thank God, whom I serve (Latreuo) with a pure conscience, as my forefathers did, as without ceasing I remember you in my prayers night and day,

Hebrews 12:28 (NKJV) Therefore, since we are receiving a kingdom which cannot be shaken, let us have grace, by which we may serve (Latreuo) God acceptably with reverence and godly fear. (Note: KJV translates this passage as "serve" instead of "worship")

Revelation 7:15 (NKJV) Therefore they are before the throne of God, and serve (Latreuo) Him day and night in His temple. And He who sits on the throne will dwell among them.

Sebomai

The third and last Greek word for "worship" in the New Testament is Sebomai. Found ten times, eight of which appear in Acts.

SEBOMAI: It means "to reverence" or "to hold in awe."
Translated as an English adjective, such as "devout," "God-fearing," or "religious."

Mark 7:6-7 (NKJV) He (Jesus) answered and said to them, "Well did Isaiah prophesy of you hypocrites, as it is written: 'This people honors Me with their lips, But their heart is far from Me. And in vain they worship (Sebomai) Me, Teaching as doctrines the commandments of men.'

Acts 13:43 (NKJV) Now when the congregation had broken up, many of the Jews and devout (KJV: Religious) (Sebomai) proselytes followed Paul and Barnabas, who, speaking to them, persuaded them to continue in the grace of God.

Acts 13:49-50 (NKJV) And the word of the Lord was being spread throughout all the region. But the Jews stirred up the devout (Sebomai) and prominent women and the chief men of the city, raised up persecution against Paul and Barnabas, and expelled them from their region.

Acts 17:16-17 (NKJV) Now while Paul waited for them at Athens, his spirit was provoked within him when he saw that the city was given over to idols. Therefore he reasoned in the synagogue with the Jews and with the Gentile worshippers (KJV: devout person() (Sebomai), and in the marketplace daily with those who happened to be there.

Our Internal Intimacy with God

Just as five of the Hebrew words had nothing to do with music, none of the Greek words refer to music either. The Hebrew words for worship primarily focused on the way the Israelites postured themselves before God: kneeling, bowing, the raising of hands, falling prostrate, etc. God looks at the heart of a man. Our worship must begin with our internal intimacy with God. The Israelites moved away from this intimacy, and their animal sacrifices became a ritual. They were just "going through the motions."

Our physical expression of worship through posture should be an outward expression of the internal position of our heart. Worship is sacramental in nature, an outward and visible expression of an inward and spiritual revelation. God reveals His goodness to us—our hearts are filled with thanksgiving, and we raise our hands externally. God reveals His majesty to us—our hearts are filled with awe and wonder, and we bow in adoration. God shows His might to us—our hearts fill with humility, and we fall prostrate before the altar.

Kneeling Before the Lord (Shachah)

When I first saw Jesus, my reaction was to bow before Him. I knew I was worshipping Him. I wanted to kneel because I was before the Lord of lords and King of kings. No one had to tell me to bow. Sometimes in the service or when praying, I kneel before Him in worship. I came to know from Heaven that this is the natural response to Jesus' presence. The other ways of showing Him worship are great, but most people who are born again want to bow or lay before Him. When you sense His presence, I encourage you to try it sometime. You are bowing because you love Him, not because others see you.

The Amazing Scene in Heaven

REVELATION 4:1-11 (NKJV)

After these things I looked, and behold, a door standing open in heaven. And the first voice, which I heard, was like a trumpet speaking with me, saying, "Come up here, and I will show you things which must take place after this." Immediately I was in the Spirit; and behold, a throne set in heaven, and One sat on the throne. And He who sat there was like a jasper and a sardius stone in appearance; and there was a rainbow around the throne, in appearance like an emerald. Around the throne were twenty-four thrones, and on the thrones, I saw twenty-four elders sitting, clothed in white robes; and they had crowns of gold on their heads. And from the throne proceeded lightnings, thunderings, and voices. Seven lamps of fire were burning before the throne, which are the seven Spirits of God. Before the throne, there was a sea of glass, like crystal. And in the midst of the throne, and around the throne, were four living creatures full of eyes in front and in back. The first living creature was like a lion, the second living creature like a calf, the third living creature had a face like a man, and the fourth living creature was like a flying eagle. The four living creatures, each having six wings, were full of eyes around and within. And they do not rest day or night, saying: "Holy, holy, holy, Lord God Almighty, Who was and is and is to come!" Whenever the living creatures give glory and honor and thanks to Him who sits on the throne, who lives forever and ever, the twenty-four elders fall down before Him who sits on the throne and worship Him who lives forever and ever, and cast their crowns before the throne, saying: "You are worthy, O Lord, To receive glory and honor and power; For You created all things, And by Your will they exist and were created."

So, here we see the picture around the Throne of what is going on all the time. Now, this next picture is what happened around the Throne while I was there.

The Opening of the Scroll

REVELATION 5:1-14 (NKJV)

And I saw in the right hand of Him who sat on the throne
a scroll written inside and on the back, sealed with seven
seals. Then I saw a strong angel proclaiming with a loud voice,
"Who is worthy to open the scroll and to loose its seals?" And
no one in heaven or on the earth or under the earth was able
to open the scroll, or to look at it. So I wept much, because
no one was found worthy to open and read the scroll, or to
look at it. But one of the elders said to me, "Do not weep.
Behold, the Lion of the tribe of Judah, the Root of David, has
prevailed to open the scroll and to loose its seven seals." And I
looked, and behold, in the midst of the throne and of the four
living creatures, and in the midst of the elders, stood a Lamb
as though it had been slain, having seven horns and seven
eyes, which are the seven Spirits of God sent out into all the
earth. Then He came and took the scroll out of the right hand
of Him who sat on the throne. Now when He had taken the
scroll, the four living creatures and the twenty-four elders fell
down before the Lamb, each having a harp, and golden bowls
full of incense, which are the prayers of the saints. And they
sang a new song, saying: "You are worthy to take the scroll,
And to open its seals; For You were slain, And have redeemed
us to God by Your blood Out of every tribe and tongue and
people and nation, And have made us kings and priests to our
God; And we shall reign on the earth." Then I looked, and I
heard the voice of many angels around the throne, the living
creatures, and the elders; and the number of them was ten
thousand times ten thousand, and thousands of thousands,

saying with a loud voice: "Worthy is the Lamb who was slain To receive power and riches and wisdom, And strength and honor and glory and blessing!" And every creature which is in heaven and on the earth and under the earth and such as are in the sea, and all that are in them, I heard saying: "Blessing and honor and glory and power Be to Him who sits on the throne, And to the Lamb, forever and ever!" Then the four living creatures said, "Amen!" And the twenty-four elders fell down and worshipped Him who lives forever and ever.

Again How to Become a Part of the Praise of Heaven

If you want to be a part of this praise in heaven, you must be born again. To do this, you have to confess with your mouth that Jesus is Lord and believe in your heart that God raised Him from the dead, and you will be saved!

Say the Following to Be Saved

Dear Father God, I ask You to forgive me for anything I have done wrong to You or others. I invite You to come and be a part of my life. I thank You for hearing me, forgiving me, and coming into my life. I give You all of my life now. I ask and declare all of this in the name of Jesus. Amen.

Hear His Song

If you said this and meant it in your heart, You Are Now Saved! You will and can praise your heavenly Father right now. SO, SING and hear Him sing to you.

ROMANS 10:8-13 (NKJV)

But what does it say? "The word is near you, in your mouth and in your heart" that is, the word of faith which we preach: that if you confess with your mouth the Lord Jesus and believe in your heart that God has raised Him from the dead, you will be saved. For with the heart one believes unto righteousness, and with the mouth confession is made unto salvation. For the Scripture says, "Whoever believes on Him will not be put to shame." For there is no distinction between Jew and Greek, for the same Lord over all is rich to all who call upon Him. For "whoever calls on the name of the Lord shall be saved."

DEEP WORSHIP

By

Mary C. E. Davis

My private chamber I entered in, and quieted my soul within

In stillness stayed… and time stood still as shadows fled, light filtered in

A sense of awe, I dared not move, as His presence filled the room

I basked a time in His embrace and sought the Glory of His face

A melody from deep within arose as an unuttered hymn

Rent veil appeared amid my soul, inviting me to deeper go

A deep foreboding in my heart did, from the entrance make me start

Confused, I stopped to ponder there and fear did try to come… despair

"My child," He softly said to me, "Safely come, abide with Me. Eternal foe, I have but one.

He, by your worship, is undone. Within his wretched soul abides the pipes and timbrels for all time,

and if he stayed within the reach of your worship, precious, sweet, the resonance of harmony would

cause his soul to worship Me. So, when to worship you had chose, this foe of Mine you did depose.

A melody so soft and sweet, as deep to deep your love for Me and so, your simple gift to me will from

your life now make him flee."

Now treasure I the times, so sweet, to enter in and with Him meet.